Cleopatra of Egypt

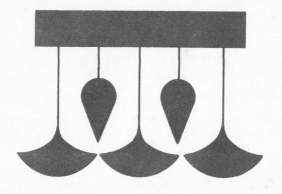

Cleopatra
OF EGYPT

by Leonora Hornblow

ILLUSTRATED BY W. T. MARS

WORLD
Landmark
BOOKS

RANDOM HOUSE, N.Y.

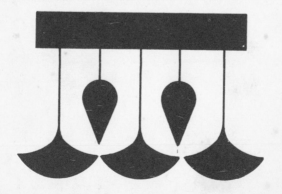

To Michael Hornblow
with love

Contents

Part Three

Author's Note

There are some people who are so extraordinary that they leave their stamp upon the world and are not ever forgotten. Cleopatra is one. Her name has become a symbol of romance and excitement and fascination.

Tales began to be told about her when she was alive and Queen of Egypt. But very little that was written by her early admirers—or her enemies—is left for us today. Nevertheless her appeal for poets and playwrights and storytellers has never ceased. The important facts about her are well recorded. But because so many others are not, legend and fancy have made their contribution over the many years.

Cleopatra became wonderfully real to me while I was working on this book. Plutarch speaks of her lovely voice. Shakespeare, who saw everything more truly than anyone else and said it better, wrote of her:

> "Age cannot wither, nor custom stale
> Her infinite variety. . . ."

When you read this book let your imagination work with mine and perhaps we can see her as she was long ago.

L.H.

Part One

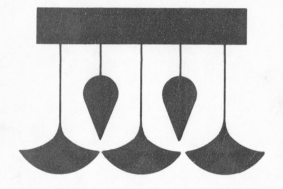

CHAPTER I

The Purple Tent

On the northern shores of Africa one bright morning in the fall of the year 48 B.C. two armies stood face to face in bitter combat. One of them was commanded by the King of Egypt, who was a boy of fifteen named Ptolemy. The other was the army of the Queen of Egypt, who was not only the wife of Ptolemy but also his sister.

It is hard to imagine a more remarkable situation: two young people who were brother and sister as well as husband and wife. Each was eager to kill the other so that the survivor might rule alone the ancient land that their father had left them to rule together.

The Queen was a bit older than her brother, just past nineteen. She was intelligent, beautiful and daring. Her name was Cleopatra, and she was going to become one of the ten most famous women who have ever lived.

Three years previously her father, King Ptolemy Auletes, had died. Cleopatra and her brother had governed Egypt together for some time. Then, six months before this day, a great quarrel had broken out.

Ptolemy's advisers hated Cleopatra because they

could not control her. They felt that she thought too much for herself. Ptolemy's high chamberlain, Pothinus, arranged for Cleopatra to be expelled from the royal palace at Alexandria, where she had lived all her life. The banished queen hid in the great desert outside Alexandria, gradually gathering support to her side. What she wanted she would fight for, and she wanted Egypt. From all over Egypt, and even from within the palace and the army, strong men joined her cause.

Pothinus was amazed. Ptolemy, who was weak, was terrified as his sister began to show her strength. His forces gathered to oppose her, and war broke out. It was civil war, which is the cruelest sort, because people of the same race and heritage shed each other's blood and devastate their own land.

This morning Cleopatra was standing in the opening of her battle tent, which was made of a rich purple material, embroidered in gold. It was a place of coolness and shade. For safety, the Queen's personal camp was well to the rear of the actual fighting. But Cleopatra would rather have been in the middle of the battle, instead of waiting impatiently for messengers to bring her news. Standing there, she looked even younger than nineteen. She was dark and slender, and when she moved she was quick and graceful. She always stood very straight. Even now in her own tent when no one could see her, she stood as she thought a queen should stand.

She had always looked forward to being Queen of Egypt. But she had also known, from early childhood, that it was not going to be easy to accomplish. Several of her father's children had been ahead of her, and she had had jealous enemies as well. But none

was more dangerous than her brother Ptolemy and his crafty chamberlain, Pothinus.

Cleopatra looked over to where the members of her staff were gathered. They sat talking with Barak, her general, beneath an awning stretched over great striped poles stuck into the sand. Like her, they waited impatiently for news of the action. It seemed to her this morning that the long days of fighting for a decision would never end. She wanted to go back to Alexandria in triumph. In Cleopatra's mind there was never any question that Egypt belonged to her. She felt this intensely even though she herself did not really belong to Egypt.

She did not even think of herself as an Egyptian, nor had any member of her family, although they had lived and ruled in Egypt for over three hundred years. Cleopatra and all her ancestors behind her were Greek. The founder of her royal line, Ptolemy I, had first come to Egypt from Macedonia, to the north of Greece. He came with Alexander the Great, who was also a Macedonian. Ptolemy had been a general in Alexander's army at the time of his great march of conquest.

After defeating the Egyptians, Alexander took possession of their country and founded a new capital which he named Alexandria after himself. He chose a spot on the edge of the Mediterranean where the green waters of the Nile flowed into the deeply blue sea.

Alexander had greatly admired the Greeks. During his lifetime—and long after—Greece was the source of art and culture and knowledge. Almost everything that was beautiful either came from Greece or was directly influenced by Greek taste. So naturally Alexander saw to it that his new city was built throughout in the Grecian style. Because of its fortunate location, Alexandria soon became the center of trade for three continents—Europe, Asia and Africa. The wealth and fame of Egypt rose rapidly.

When the famous conqueror died, his general Ptolemy seized Egypt as his share of the divided empire. Cleopatra's ancestor turned out to be a good and wise ruler, except perhaps for one thing. Because he wanted the blood of his royal line to remain Macedonian, he laid down a rule that lasted for three centuries. The rule was that Ptolemy brothers and sisters were to marry each other and keep for themselves and their offspring the right to govern.

This system gradually led not only to a weak lot of rulers but also to terrible feuds within the family itself. Because all the Ptolemies seemed to have many children, their story over the years was one of bitterness and murder. Sons murdered their fathers; sons and daughters were killed by their fathers, and there was deadly rivalry of the kind that was once again bringing disaster and death, this time to the entire country.

But somehow, despite this endless disorder, the Ptolemies had lived through the centuries in luxury and splendor. Some of them had never in their lives left Alexandria and had no idea of the vast, secret country which they ruled. But at least they continued to add to the beauty of the city with palaces, museums and lovely villas. These were built of marble in the classic style. The buildings shone white as sugar in the sun. At night they appeared to be made of the moon itself. Beautifully planted terraces were around each building; the gardens were marvels. The light, dry Egyptian air was always sweet with the smell of fruits and flowers which grew abundantly everywhere.

By the time Cleopatra was born, Alexandria was the largest and handsomest city on the Mediterranean Sea. The Lighthouse of Pharos, the noble beacon in the harbor, was one of the seven wonders of the world. The library might well have been considered a wonder too. It contained hundreds of thousands of rolls of papyrus that recorded man's history to that time, as well as all his learning. Nothing could compare with this collection.

The scholars who came from all over the world to study at the library were frequently heard to say that Cleopatra was the first of her family for many generations to have the character and charm of Ptolemy I. He had been an ambitious and cruel man, but a learned and brilliant one as well. Most of his descendants had just been cruel.

As Cleopatra stood in the entry of the purple tent, she heard the sound of a galloping horse. A mounted messenger was pulling up at the edge of the royal enclosure. He identified himself to the guard and walked swiftly toward the group gathered around General Barak.

Cleopatra watched for a moment, then turned and called, "Charmian!"

Almost instantly from behind a fold of the tent there emerged a lovely-looking girl. She was taller than Cleopatra, darker and of about the same age. This was the Queen's favorite lady in waiting, one of the few people she trusted in her world of plotters and spies.

"I am here, Divinity."

Cleopatra looked off again, this time impatiently, at
the group that was listening to the messenger. "Tell
Madrian to find out the news the messenger has
brought."

"At once," answered Charmian. She clapped her
hands together twice, then again twice. That was the
signal to Madrian that he was wanted. But he did not
appear.

Madrian was a tiny man with a big round head.
No one knew how old he was. He still looked exactly
the same as he did the day he arrived at the royal
palace. He had been sent several years before to Cleopatra's father by his brother, the King of Cyprus.
Since then Cyprus had become a province of Rome
and Cleopatra's uncle had killed himself. But Madrian
remained in Egypt.

He had greatly amused Ptolemy Auletes and had
been useful to him. Because he was so very small and
agile, Madrian could hide in many places. He had become a valuable spy. In spite of his size, his strength
was amazing.

When Cleopatra was still a little girl, Madrian had
dreamed that she would someday be Queen of Egypt.
From that moment on he was constantly with her
wherever she went. By his daring and his talent for
finding out things, he had twice saved Cleopatra's life.

When he did not respond to the summons, Charmian wondered where he was. She moved around the
wall of the tent, again clapping her hands. Then suddenly she saw him, darting toward her from the other
direction.

"There you are, you little beast!"

Madrian grinned. "I was well occupied."

"The Queen wishes you to find out immediately what word the messenger brought. Go!"

"Why go to do what I have done already?" Madrian replied. "I was behind the General, listening, while you stood here clapping your pretty hands."

Despite herself, Charmian smiled. "Then present yourself inside at once to Her Majesty."

Madrian moved quickly toward the entry of the tent. Then, as he was about to enter, he turned again to Charmian.

"I shall do as you bid. But the news will not make her happy."

CHAPTER II

The Messengers

Inside the tent, Cleopatra reclined on linen cushions. An attendant, Iras, was fanning her while the Queen sipped cool wine from a golden cup. The day was becoming warm.

Madrian ran into the tent and flung himself on the ground. "Divinity," the little man began. "Priceless Treasure of the Earth!"

"Be still, Madrian!" Cleopatra commanded. "I know who I am. Tell me what you have found out. Tell me quickly."

"As you wish, Exalted One," said Madrian in an offended tone. "The messenger you saw——"

"I know I saw him, fool," Cleopatra interrupted. "Get on with it, will you."

Madrian half hesitated. Then he went on. "Our cavalry has met Ptolemy's near Pelusium——"

Cleopatra sat up. "Yes?"

"Nothing. Bad losses on both sides and then retreat."

Cleopatra meditated on this, her face expressionless.

"But there is one piece of good news at least," Madrian continued. "The messenger reports that your brother the king was sick again last night. Today he

is too weak to take food or sit upon his horse."

"That's good." Cleopatra smiled. "Anything else?"

"Nothing, Divinity. No progress in the battle at any point."

Cleopatra stood up, her face stormy. "The battle could go on like this for weeks—for months. If I were a man I would be in the fight myself. My soldiers need a leader!"

While Cleopatra was speaking, Charmian entered the tent. The Queen looked at her.

"I would fight from a light chariot in the midst of the battle. As *he* fought! Do you remember, Charmian?"

"Who, Your Majesty?"

"The Roman. The handsome one who came with the Roman legions to help my father regain his throne from my sister Berenice."

Charmian smiled and sighed. "There were so many handsome Roman soldiers, Majesty."

"But none like him. He was commander of their cavalry. Tall and brown—and descended from Hercules, they said. He used to walk in the garden in the evenings with his friends. I would sit in my window and listen to him laugh."

"What was his name, Divinity? Do you remember?"

"He was called Mark Antony. Do you not remember him now?"

"*I* do!" cried out Madrian, always unable to keep quiet when the talk was interesting to him.

Cleopatra turned slowly to regard him. "What do you know about Mark Antony?"

"He was fearless, Beautiful Queen, and his men loved him. When they were here four years ago, they told endless stories of his bravery and his skill in battle. They say that he is a great friend of the mighty Julius Caesar."

Charmian shivered. "I remember it all well. You were a prisoner in the palace before he came. Oh, when I think of those dreadful days I feel sick."

"Then don't think of them," said Cleopatra. "My sister Berenice is dead as she well deserves to be."

She moved again to the opening of her tent and looked out over the smooth sands. Four years earlier, when Mark Antony came to Alexandria, she had still been a child. For a while she had indeed been a prisoner of her terrible sister. Berenice had seized the throne of her father during his absence from Egypt. Then Antony, on instructions from Rome, had entered Egypt and restored Auletes to power.

Cleopatra had seen him many times. He had smiled

at her, talked to her pleasantly, but he hadn't really noticed her.

"I wonder if Mark Antony will ever come back to Egypt," said Charmian softly, voicing the very thoughts of the Queen. The breeze from the desert blew her words away, but not before Madrian heard them.

"The soothsayer can tell us," he began, "I will——"

But before he could finish, Iras approached to say that another messenger had arrived and that General Barak was on the way to see the Queen with urgent news.

Cleopatra went forward to meet him. Barak was blunt, strong and immensely loyal. What he had to report was unexpected and startling. Word had come that the great Roman general, Julius Caesar, was at that moment entering the harbor of Alexandria with a fleet and a large body of men. He had defeated his powerful rival, Pompey, in a battle on the coast of Greece. They had fought to determine who was to be master of the Roman empire. And now Caesar was descending upon Egypt!

"Where is Pompey?" Cleopatra asked, after she had heard Barak's information.

"He escaped from Greece by ship and is heading for Pelusium to ask for your brother's help. That could be the reason for Caesar's entry into Alexandria."

Suddenly another messenger was seen entering the camp. This one was a high-ranking Egyptian officer, accompanied by aides. He brought the most interesting news of all, and had been sent by Julius Caesar himself.

Caesar had already landed in Alexandria with a number of legions. Upon learning of the bitter situa-

BRITAIN

GAUL

Munda

SPAIN

Rome
Ostia

ITALY

SICILY

Mediterran

AFRICA

Cleopatra's World

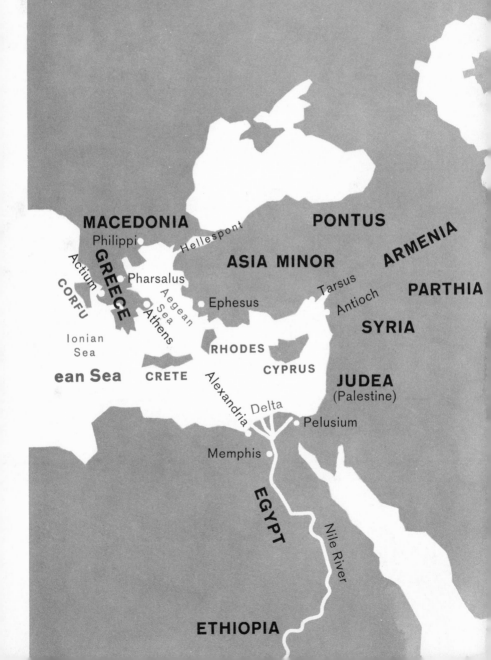

MACEDONIA

Philippi

GREECE

Actium

Pharsalus

CORFU

Athens

Aegean
Sea

Ionian
Sea

ean Sea

CRETE

Hellespont

ASIA MINOR

Ephesus

RHODES

Alexandria

PONTUS

ARMENIA

Tarsus

Antioch

PARTHIA

SYRIA

CYPRUS

JUDEA
(Palestine)

Delta

Pelusium

Memphis

EGYPT

Nile River

ETHIOPIA

tion in the royal family, he declared himself to be displeased with the fighting in Egypt and ordered it to cease. He sent the royal brother and sister his greetings and demanded that they be escorted to Alexandria as soon as possible. He wished to see Ptolemy and Cleopatra together and put an end to their feud.

To everyone's surprise, Cleopatra laughed. "Great Caesar has conquered Pompey," she said, "not Egypt!" Barak and the others knew that when she said Egypt she meant Cleopatra.

Without hesitation the Queen turned to Barak and spoke to him softly so that they would not be overheard by the others.

"I will go myself," she said. "I will see Caesar in my own way. I do not need to be conducted to him in my own country."

"But he has said that he wants to meet with you and your brother at the same time," Barak warned.

"I intend to see him *alone*," Cleopatra replied. "I want to see him before Ptolemy and Pothinus do. We have word that Ptolemy is sick. He won't travel today."

"When will you leave for Alexandria, Majesty?"

"Immediately!" said Cleopatra.

CHAPTER III

The Journey to Alexandria

Once Cleopatra made up her mind to do something she did it without delay. She was soon ready to leave the camp on the plains. Charmian gave her a little casket which held some of her jewels. Iras wrapped a light shawl around her. As Cleopatra looked around the purple tent, she hoped that she was seeing it for the last time.

Charmian was to remain in the tent, lying on the Queen's linen pillows. This was a trick to fool Ptolemy's spies. Madrian would stay with Iras and Charmian. The only member of Cleopatra's court who was to go with her was her huge Sicilian slave, Apollodorus. He had been loyal and devoted to Cleopatra ever since she was born. He was immensely tall with a great chest and broad shoulders, and there was nothing that he couldn't lift or move. Tiny Madrian was jealous of him, not only because he was so big but because the Queen liked and trusted him.

Cleopatra did not reveal her plan to anyone. She said merely that she would take as a gift for Caesar the beautiful oriental rug that covered the floor of her tent. Apollodorus rolled it up and slung it across the side of a heavy chariot at the rear of the tent. When

it was tied and set, the Queen joined him quickly and the two white steeds were lashed into action.

As the horses' hoofbeats faded in the distance, Madrian realized that he was to be left behind. Bursting into tears, he jumped up and down like a little monkey, and finally ran to Iras to hide his head in her lap.

Cleopatra and Apollodorus went directly to a small village on a branch of the River Nile not many miles from Pelusium. From there the trip to Alexandria would not be a very long one. Cleopatra had decided the river would be safer than the overland route. Once they were aboard a small boat, it would be impossible to find them. There were many places along the shore to hide, in case Ptolemy heard she was on her way to the capital.

They were able to find a fast little fishing boat, just large enough for Cleopatra, Apollodorus and the carpet. As Apollodorus pushed off from the bank and the slender, slanting red sail caught the evening breeze, Cleopatra's thoughts turned to Julius Caesar and his native land, Rome, the most powerful country on earth.

Since the middle of the third century B.C. the rule of Rome had gradually spread over the entire Mediterranean area. By the time Cleopatra's father came to the throne of Egypt, Rome's influence throughout every land that bordered on the sea was tremendous. Many of the lands that had once been mighty kingdoms had become provinces, paying homage and taxes to distant Rome.

The dreaded Roman legions straddled not only the Mediterranean but also much of Europe, such as Spain and the area called Gaul, known today as France. Cleopatra had heard that Julius Caesar was even planning the conquest of Britain, those chilly islands in the distant north.

To the Queen it seemed as if the whole known world was working for the benefit and wealth of Rome. Nor did Rome give back learning and beauty as Athens and Greece had done long ago. The Roman pattern was one of war and trade. Their only aims were conquest and gain.

Egypt alone had remained independent. But for how long? It was a question Cleopatra often asked herself. Rome made no secret of wanting to annex Egypt with all its riches and treasures. The Queen knew, as her father and grandfather had known, that Rome was waiting for an excuse to move into Egypt.

Cleopatra had to admit that her father, weak as he had been in many ways, had done a good job of keeping Egypt free of Roman rule. He had used bribery with large sums of money to accomplish this. It was an expensive method, but it had worked.

Ptolemy Auletes had gone to Rome often. Sometimes he had stayed away from Alexandria for years. It was during one of these absences that his daughter Berenice seized the throne and had herself crowned. But when the King returned, her forces had been defeated and she herself put to death.

Cleopatra well remembered sitting in the window niche of the small palace room where she had been held prisoner when she was a little girl. She would watch the great harbor, hoping for the sight of her father's sail, knowing that someday it would come.

After Ptolemy Auletes died, Cleopatra found out that he owed enormous sums to many Roman officials and persons of importance. He had pledged them the money in return for their exerting influence to keep Rome out of Egypt. Among these debts was one to Julius Caesar, and Cleopatra wondered if Caesar would now expect her to pay. She was angry at Rome. The senate had recognized her simple-minded brother as a rightful monarch at a time when they could have stopped him.

Cleopatra hated to be in the position of begging help from Rome as her father had done, but there seemed no other course. She was also annoyed at the peremptory way Caesar had summoned her to a meeting. Her only comfort was that she was arriving unknown to Caesar and in her own way.

The sun had long set, and the stars glistened and seemed within the reach of her arm in the black vel-

CHAPTER IV

A Surprise for Caesar

By dusk the following day, Cleopatra and Apollodorus reached Alexandria. The journey had been long, but the Queen was too excited to be tired. Apollodorus steered to a remote edge of the port, and they waited for the dark.

The harbor was crowded with newly anchored ships. They came from ports far and near: India, Arabia, China and Central Africa. They were waiting for their cargoes to be unloaded and stored in the warehouses of the city. In their holds were wines, ivory, spices and rare fruits. Egyptian ships were at their moorings, being made ready to leave with the morning tide. They were laden with grain and papyrus, as well as the ornaments, glassware and glazed earthenware produced in Egypt and prized the world over.

Also waiting were the strong-looking galleys of the Roman fleet. These were the ships of Caesar.

Cleopatra had only a quick glimpse of the harbor. She dared not take a chance of being seen and recognized. By now her brother's spies might have discovered that she was not at her camp. They might already be out looking for her. She curled up in the bottom of the boat, and Apollodorus covered her with the carpet.

She could smell the fine salty smell of the sea, which she had so missed on the desert. The familiar, wonderful sounds of this busy waterway delighted her. The longest part of the journey was safely behind them, but the most important part was still ahead. Cleopatra patiently waited, feeling the boat rock gently under her. She would have liked to use this time to rehearse Apollodorus again in what he must say, but she did not want to make a sound.

Then Apollodorus whispered, "I see no one near, Divinity. It is safe to go now."

"I am ready," Cleopatra said.

Following her instructions, he rolled the carpet completely around her, until she had vanished within it. Tiny openings were left at each end for air to come through. Then he bound it with cords at each of its long ends and raised it carefully to his powerful shoulder.

Looking carefully about him to make sure he had not been observed, Apollodorus stepped out of the boat. Then carrying his precious load with the greatest ease, he moved toward the center of the city.

He walked along the broad avenues that led to the royal palace. Alexandria was at that time the only city in the world which had been planned so that its streets ran at right angles to each other. Even in Rome and Athens the streets were no more than twisting, unpaved lanes.

This early evening the streets were full of people, and no one took any special notice of a tall man carrying a big rug. The taverns along the water front

were crowded too. The presence of Caesar and his
soldiers had made the Alexandrians curious and uneasy. They did not know what was going to happen.
Their two rulers, Cleopatra and Ptolemy, were away
fighting each other. Did the sudden arrival of the
powerful Julius Caesar mean that Egypt was, at last,
going to be annexed to Rome?

The population of Alexandria was a mixed one:
Greeks, Syrians, Jews, Armenians, Persians, Nubians
were among the many foreign nationalities that had
settled there. They all seemed to be outside their
houses this autumn evening, exchanging rumors. Cleopatra, hidden within the rug, could hear the things
being said. She understood almost all of these tongues,
including all the Egyptian dialects.

Apollodorus was walking fast, and soon they drew
near the royal palace.

Luck was with them. Apollodorus, clearly unarmed
and wearing his badge of slave, had no trouble in getting by the Roman sentries who were guarding the
outer circle of Caesar's quarters. Then he passed
Ptolemy's guards, who were still in the palace and
whom he had more reason to fear.

His method was simple. He asked, loud and clear, to
be taken to Caesar so that he could present him with
a gift he was bearing from the King. He was allowed
to proceed, and a guard was sent with him to conduct
him to the inner quarters.

Apollodorus followed the guard down the long,
familiar halls. Caesar was living in the royal apart-
ments, the part of the palace where Cleopatra's rooms
had been.

"Stop here!" the guard finally instructed.

They waited in front of high ebony doors until another sentry called an officer of the guard. Apollodorus stated his mission. There was a long discussion, but Apollodorus remained resolute. Inside the rug Cleopatra, who could hear all, felt her heart beat faster.

Finally the puzzled officer struck a special signal on the great doors, and they opened slightly to admit him. Bidding Apollodorus to wait, the Roman officer went inside.

Caesar was lying on one of the luxurious couches which were everywhere in the palace. He was reading, rather sleepily, a roll of papyrus from the library. One of his staff had thought it might interest him as it dealt with the Egyptian campaign of Alexander, but he was finding it dull. He knew more about that campaign than the scholar who had written the history of it.

Caesar looked up at once as the guard officer approached and smartly saluted with his right arm upraised.

"General, there is a Sicilian slave outside who asks personal audience. He is the bearer of a carpet from the King of Egypt. A most unusual carpet, he claims."

"Let us see this carpet," said Caesar. "Bring it in."

"He has been instructed to let no one else touch it, sir."

Caesar hesitated a moment, then seeming somewhat amused, he answered, "I like the sound of him. He may bring it in himself."

The General put aside the scroll and looked up again, curious to see his gift. He saw an enormous man walking slowly toward him carrying a long bundle. Apollodorus stopped, fell to one knee and in-

clined his head respectfully. Caesar waited. Then Apollodorus set the bundle down before him, loosened the cords and quickly unrolled the carpet.

In one light, graceful movement Cleopatra rose from the carpet. As she stood before Julius Caesar at last, she beheld a man quite unlike what she had expected. This was no arrogant conqueror. Instead, his face, although proud, seemed thoughtful. And he was no longer young.

Caesar simply stared at her for a moment. He was astonished as well as delighted by the sight before him —a slim young girl in a yellow silk dress crumpled from the carpet. She wore sandals and no jewelry except small earrings and one wide band of soft gold around

her upper arm. But she stood straight and proud. Her great dark eyes looked directly at him and they were shining.

Caesar was a gifted man, with great powers of insight. The bearing of this lovely young woman told him instantly who she must be. He knew that this simply dressed goddess who had arrived without ceremony or announcement was the Queen of Egypt. He had heard about her, of course, but he had thought that any woman on a battlefield must be some sort of Amazon. There were no portraits of her in the palace. Ptolemy had had them put away. So Caesar had not been prepared for anyone so beautiful—or so daring.

He rose from the couch and held out his hand with its heavy signet ring. He smiled at her, and his stern face was suddenly bright and pleased and amused.

Cleopatra gave him her own ringless hand and returned his smile. He had not yet spoken a word to her, but she was confident. He was not angry. He was charmed. The trick had worked.

CHAPTER V

The Fateful Meeting

A few minutes after Cleopatra emerged from the rug, she was sitting beside Caesar, talking to him as if they had known each other always. Caesar dismissed his guards, and Cleopatra gave Apollodorus a sign that all was well and he might leave.

On a low table near Caesar there was a golden plate heaped with fruit. The Queen had heard that he liked beautiful objects and wanted to be surrounded by them. There was a story that he always had a floor made of woven silver taken onto the field of battle for his tent. Now that she saw him, Cleopatra believed the story.

She nibbled some fresh figs of which she was very fond. There had been none in the desert. And Caesar poured wine for them both into the royal Egyptian beakers, which were tall and golden and studded with emeralds.

He asked many questions as they sipped the wine. He was especially interested in her strategy of being smuggled into the palace and was delighted by her tale of her two-day journey. As he listened admiringly, it seemed to him that Cleopatra's voice was one of the softest and loveliest he had ever heard. He thought he would never tire of the charm and cleverness of her conversation.

As for Cleopatra, she was finding Caesar more interesting and impressive than she had expected. She was used to thinking of Romans as barbarians. Even Mark Antony, the handsomest man she had ever seen, was rough. Gnaeus Pompey, the dead general's son, whom she had once met, was a pleasant companion but he was bored by reading or any of the arts. Caesar, it was plain to see, was a man of wisdom and wide interests, as well as a remarkable military leader.

She admired the air of strength and command about him. He had a well-shaped head and a strong, high-bridged nose. His brow and his firm cheeks were burned by the sun and wind to a deep coppery color. His eyes were black, deep-set. It seemed to Cleopatra that no secret was safe from those black eyes. But she saw kindness—even gentleness—in them as he looked at her.

Caesar behaved as if he were the host at the palace. But neither of them forgot that the palace belonged to Cleopatra by inheritance. It was an inheritance she intended to preserve.

He, on the other hand, had inherited nothing. He had worked and fought to attain his high position. But it was still not high enough for him. His ambition was boundless. Ever since boyhood he had been influenced by Alexander the Great and his exploits. As he sat now in Alexander's city, his wish for absolute power was stronger than ever.

Caesar and Cleopatra talked of many things, but she was disappointed that nothing was really decided.

Nevertheless one thing, at least, encouraged her. She had plenty of chance to tell her side of the situation that existed in Egypt. Caesar listened closely. He went so far as to admit that he disliked and distrusted Pothinus, holding him responsible for the treacherous murder of Pompey. He realized fully that the act was to gain his favor; instead it had gained his disgust.

Cleopatra asked if he were going to see Ptolemy. Caesar revealed that the young king was expected to arrive the following morning.

"He will be surprised to find me here." Cleopatra laughed as she spoke.

Caesar smiled in agreement, then told her he would order her rooms and her person to be well guarded. Cleopatra thanked him, though she wished that he would consult her instead of giving orders. But seeing that he did not care to pursue with her now the matter of the struggle within Egypt, she refrained from pressing him. Instead she rose to bid him good night.

When Cleopatra was once again back in her own room, she looked contentedly out of her window at the harbor. The gleaming beacon light of Pharos glowed in the darkness. It seemed to shine a welcome to her. Across the dark water were the other countries of the world. As a child she had sat in this very window and imagined sailing from Alexandria to Greece and then on to Rome. Perhaps now, at last, she would.

On the other side of the sea was Julius Caesar's world, and he would be returning to it. He was free to leave any time he wanted to; his ships awaited him. But somehow Cleopatra felt that he was not going to hurry away from Alexandria. Their meeting had been fateful she was sure. Even though he had said nothing definite, she sensed that he would be on her side.

"He is remarkable," she thought. Then she fell back contentedly on her silken bed. The perfume of the gardens filled her room. The moon set. Cleopatra was sleeping, no longer afraid of tomorrow.

CHAPTER VI

One Voice and Many Voices

The next morning Cleopatra had a bath. Her marble tub was filled with warm and perfumed water from the Nile. It was in a room by itself next to her bedchamber.

After her bath, she dressed with great care. She had heard that the ladies of Rome were elegant and paid careful attention to their clothes and jewels and how their hair was arranged. She did not wish Caesar to compare her with them to her disadvantage.

It was good to be back among all her lovely things. Instead of the sandals she had worn in the desert, she put on fine shoes. Her hair was brushed with perfume and hung to her shoulders in soft curls. She reddened her lips with lees of wine. Around her eyelids she drew lines with kohl, a cosmetic that is still in use. When she had put on a heavy necklace and long earrings she was ready to greet Caesar in the great hall.

He was dazzled by her splendor and her beauty. She seemed altogether different from the young girl of last night. He was to learn that one of the most captivating things about her was that her variety was endless. Because she was easily bored, she could never stand the idea that she might bore anybody.

Cleopatra noticed with pleasure that Caesar had ordered her portraits and likenesses to be reinstalled in the palace. He had learned that they had been removed by order of Ptolemy when she fled from the palace in fear for her life.

At last Ptolemy was announced. Cleopatra stepped back into the shadows of the great hall, sitting on an alabaster bench to watch the proceedings. Ptolemy entered, dressed in regal attire. He was followed by members of his staff, including Pothinus. On his head he wore a small crown, token of his rank.

Pothinus, it seemed to Cleopatra, was oilier than ever. He fawned on both Ptolemy and Caesar and gave lying excuses for the death of Pompey, which Caesar pretended to believe. She listened carefully to what they were saying, waiting to make her presence known. The moment came soon.

Ptolemy announced to Caesar that it was his immediate intention to return to the battlefield. He intended to destroy his sister's forces before the month was ended. Pothinus added that there was no other course to follow, since Cleopatra had amply proved her unworthiness to rule with her brother.

At this, Cleopatra decided to show herself. She did not say anything. She just moved out of the shadow from behind a pillar and quietly sat down beside Julius Caesar.

Ptolemy turned nearly purple when he saw her. Uttering every curse he could think of at his sister, he flung off his little crown and stamped on it with rage. He had to be forcibly held back from strangling her.

Throughout this display, Cleopatra sat quietly and

stared at him coldly. Caesar also said nothing, but waited.

Pothinus did his best to calm the King. He was too clever to reveal his own shock at seeing Cleopatra on such evidently friendly terms with the great Roman.

Ptolemy pushed Pothinus aside and ran out of the hall, screaming that he had been betrayed. Pothinus ran after him. He was afraid that if he didn't catch Ptolemy the young king might throw himself out of one of the high windows.

Cleopatra watched with interest and amusement.

"He has not changed at all," she finally said, "and Pothinus is just as evil."

There was silence for a moment as Caesar weighed the situation. Then he said, "They seem a curious pair of fish!"

He was tempted to say more, but he could not promise Cleopatra the kingdom, however fascinated he was by her. His business was to create peace in Egypt, because for the moment that would best serve Rome. If Cleopatra was disappointed, she was careful not to show it. Though Caesar was now in a position of total power, she was still the Queen of Egypt and would behave accordingly.

They became aware of a loud noise outside the palace. An officer came in to say that a large mob was gathering. They were angry because they had heard that their young king had been insulted by Caesar. They also were expressing resentment at the presence in Alexandria of so many armed Roman soldiers.

Caesar rose. "Pothinus works quickly," he said.

Cleopatra then saw Caesar in a way she was never to forget. He asked the guard for his personal armor.

When he had it on, he went to one of the tall open windows from which the noisy crowd could behold him clearly. He stood there looking out at them with a steady, searching gaze until they had quieted.

He spoke plainly and clearly with his commander's voice that could be heard at the far reaches of the square. He told them he had come not to harm but to help Egypt, that he wished to restore peace and would do so. He declared there would be a public meeting the following day and that everything would be explained at that time. Until then he expected them to preserve order and quiet in the streets. In fact he demanded it. He didn't speak of his authority and his strength, but he left no doubt in their minds that he had it. The mob quietly broke up. Some of them asked by what right this Roman intruded into the affairs of their country, but most were willing to accept what he had said.

Caesar watched for a time, then turned away from the window and met the look of admiration in Cleopatra's eyes. But he did not linger in his enjoyment of her admiration. Instead he issued orders for his high staff officers that Ptolemy should be either invited or dragged to the public meeting tomorrow. Pothinus was also to be there, as well as any other followers Ptolemy might want in attendance. Caesar instructed special guards to make certain that neither the King nor his henchmen be permitted to leave the palace that night.

Cleopatra, seeing little Madrian quietly enter the hall, called him from his hiding place and learned that he had just arrived with Charmian and Iras from the desert. The Queen, pleased to have him back, told him not to let Pothinus out of his sight.

This done, Caesar shed his cloak of authority and turned to Cleopatra with a smile. He was letting her get hungry, he said, and did she not think that some quail roasted on a spit would make an excellent meal. He would present his own troops to her later in the day.

Cleopatra agreed that his plan was excellent, and willingly accepted both the quail and the prospect of reviewing his troops. Life had suddenly become extremely peaceful. Ptolemy's screaming was over, at least for the day. The angry voices outside were silent. The doubting voice within her was silent, too.

CHAPTER VII

Peace for a Time

Before the public meeting the next morning, Caesar and Ptolemy met privately, without Pothinus. The high chamberlain was insulted and furious, but there was nothing he could do about it. Ptolemy had somewhat recovered from his shock at seeing his sister on such good terms with Caesar. He was glad to be back in the palace again. He didn't like fighting battles, and he hated being away from Alexandria.

Caesar was able quickly to convince Ptolemy to make peace with his sister. He could be both persuasive and tactful when he wanted to be. This morning he chose to flatter the young king. Ptolemy found the great soldier gravely asking his opinion about things. Pothinus had warned Ptolemy that Caesar would threaten him, but there was no sign of this. Before an hour had passed, Ptolemy had agreed that Cleopatra should rule jointly with him once again.

The Queen was waiting in the adjoining room. At Caesar's signal she came in. The two enemies spoke to each other quietly for the first time in six months. Caesar had made Cleopatra promise the day before that she would not taunt her brother.

They proceeded together into the large meeting hall with a fanfare of trumpets. The assembled supporters of both sides seemed at first sullen and resentful. Then Caesar read Ptolemy Auletes' will to them, one that he had written in Rome. This was a surprise. In the will, Auletes had left all his children under the guidance and protection ·of Rome. For this reason, Caesar explained, he had come to Egypt to make certain his old friend's wishes were fulfilled.

Perhaps it was convenient, on this occasion, for Caesar to forget that he had really been in pursuit of Pompey, especially since his former great rival was now dead. He went on to declare that, as a gesture of friendship, the Island of Cyprus would be returned to Egypt. For many years it had been a Roman province.

This promptly changed the hostile mood of the gathering. Cheers went up as Caesar went on to announce that Cyprus would be ruled by the two younger children of Ptolemy Auletes—Cleopatra's younger sister and brother, a girl named Arsinoë who was seventeen, and a boy of eleven.

There were more cheers after this. Caesar held up his hand for silence. The best news he had saved for the last. Their majesties Ptolemy XIII and Cleopatra would again rule together as their father had wished. He declared that the war between them was at an end, and that there would be a great feast on the following night to celebrate the new peace in Egypt.

The meeting ended on a note of relief and satisfaction at this outcome, for most of the people wished for peace. But among the hundreds present, four people remained deeply dissatisfied with what they had heard. One of these, of course, was Pothinus. He was well aware that Cleopatra hated him and would not overlook a chance for revenge at his having turned her out of the palace. Pothinus was disgusted with Ptolemy. The young king had done exactly what Pothinus had warned him not to do. Pothinus felt the future was threatening to them both.

There was also Arsinoë. She had no love for her brother Ptolemy, but she preferred him to her sister the Queen. Cleopatra had once remarked that Arsinoë was exactly like a "little Berenice." Arsinoë resented this. She knew that she was better looking than their older sister Berenice, and not so clumsy. But it was true that she shared one powerful drive with Berenice —ambition. To rule Cyprus was not enough for Arsinoë. It had long been her secret intention to rule Egypt itself. If Ptolemy and Cleopatra didn't kill each other, she would manage somehow to do away with both of them. The curse of the Ptolemy blood was about to show itself in Arsinoë.

Cleopatra's young sister had a tutor named Ganymede. She had not wanted a tutor, nor did she share the Queen's interest in books and science. She had always refused to join Cleopatra in her studies until she saw Ganymede one day. He was good-looking and she immediately fell in love with him.

Ganymede had decided that Arsinoë presented him with a chance to become rich and powerful. Cyprus did not fit in with his dreams of glory. So he, like Arsinoë, resented being exiled with her to what they regarded as a dreary island.

The fourth malcontent was perhaps the most surprising of all. He was a Roman officer named Achillas

who had been living in Alexandria for some time in
charge of the small Roman garrison there. He had
been secretly sent by some elements in the Roman
senate to help Ptolemy fight Cleopatra. They wanted
to eliminate a strong queen in order to advance their
own fortunes with a weak king. Also Achillas had always feared and distrusted Caesar.

These, then, were the four people who resented
Caesar's proclamation. Ptolemy, for the moment at
least, appeared pacified by Caesar's words and the
promise of freedom from Roman intrusion. Pothinus,
aware of the feelings of the other three, determined
that he would gather them together in revolt.

Cleopatra intended to make the banquet on the following night the most magnificent that Caesar had
ever attended. By now all her attendants and slaves
were back at the palace with her. She carefully made
her plans to show Caesar the grandeur and luxury of
Egypt.

The room where the banquet was held was as big
as a temple. The walls were of carved marble and
ivory. The floor was black and shining and slippery.
The ceiling beams were covered with pure gold.

The hundred guests dined at long tables made of
ivory. Each goblet and each plate was of gold. The
parade of food was endless: birds and fish of every
kind; lamb roasted on a spit the way the Greeks
cooked it. Heads of sheep were baked with apples,
which was a favorite dish in Rome. Stews appeared
made of all kinds of exotic sea food from the Mediterranean. This was an Egyptian specialty.

Cleopatra had found out that Caesar's favorite food
was mushrooms, so she had managed to obtain some.

There were all kinds of wine to drink, as well as fruits served soaked in wine. For every guest there was a crown to wear made of spikenard and roses. Everyone ate and drank and listened to the music and seemed to be enjoying the brilliant occasion.

Caesar was seated on a low couch at one end of the hall, between the King and the Queen. Cleopatra wore jewels of an oriental splendor such as Caesar had never seen in his life. Her robe was pale green in color and nearly transparent. It was the color of the Nile, she said.

As the meal was drawing to a close, Caesar rose to speak. He said that in all his travels he had never seen a land so beautiful or fascinating as Egypt. He wanted to learn all that he could about this country. He wanted to study the inscriptions on the temples and palaces built so many years ago by the Pharaohs, the ancient kings who had ruled for long centuries before the Ptolemies.

Above all, declared Caesar, he wanted to seek the source of the great and mysterious river Nile. There was a gasp from the audience at that. To say that he was going to find the source of the Nile was the same as saying he intended to do the impossible.

"I shall find it," Caesar insisted. "I shall drink the waters of the Nile at their beginning."

No one there believed him except Cleopatra. She was ready to believe that he could do anything.

At the banquet Pothinus set his scheme to work. Under the cover of the music and the feasting he was able to speak to Achillas and Ganymede. Before the long and gay evening had ended, Pothinus had already planted seeds of new war in the soil of the new peace.

The days of harmony which followed the banquet were pleasant for Caesar and Cleopatra. They went all over the city together. Caesar had spoken sincerely when he talked about studying the old buildings and monuments, and Cleopatra had always been interested in the great structures the Pharaohs had left, including the remarkable pyramids they had built to serve as their own tombs.

One day they rode out to see the Temple of Serapis. To reach it they had to climb a hundred steps. Rising high on top of a hill, the massive temple towered over the busy city. Another afternoon she took him to see the tomb of Alexander. This was an unforgettable experience for Caesar. Alexander was his hero, and he had patterned his life and his career on Alexander's.

The famous conqueror's body was in a crystal coffin. Originally it had been wrapped in sheets of heavy gold but these had disappeared long before. When the heavy lid of the casket was raised, Caesar could make out through the ancient glass the shape of Alexander's remains wrapped in the fine linen that had been used for burials three hundred years before.

Nearly every day Caesar and Cleopatra went to the library. It was enormous, high and airy. Light streamed through many windows onto the hundreds of thousands of rolls of papyrus. These rolls were in open cabinets, easy to reach. The titles were written on tickets that hung at the end of every shelf. Each subject was in its own section, as our libraries are arranged to this day. Caesar admired it and resolved to improve Rome's libraries to match it.

In the autumn evenings, which were still warm, they sat in the gardens while they talked and read together.

They liked to read the Greek tragedies aloud and sometimes to act bits for each other.

During this time Caesar told Cleopatra much about his early days and his battles. She asked many questions about his life. He told her about his friend Brutus who had fought against him with Pompey. When Pompey met disaster at Pharsalus, Caesar had spared Brutus' life because of their old friendship.

They spoke also about Mark Antony. Caesar was fond of him and amused by him. But Cleopatra no longer thought of Antony as she had before. There was no room in her thoughts for anyone but Caesar.

Reluctantly Caesar realized that he must think of returning to Rome. His men were growing restless. Because of his many battles Caesar had been away from Rome for years except for very short visits. He was aware that he must now take advantage of Pompey's defeat by returning in triumph and reminding the people of what he had done.

But somehow he could not bear the idea of leaving Egypt and the beautiful queen. He put off making a decision until, as often happens, it was made for him. The pleasant days of peace ended suddenly and soon.

CHAPTER VIII

The Alexandrian War

While Cleopatra and Caesar were happily exploring the city, Pothinus had not been idle. There were several secret meetings with Achillas, Arsinoë and Ganymede. King Ptolemy was still living in the palace as though he were Caesar's guest, well treated and free to do as he liked. But Pothinus circulated the rumor that Ptolemy was not being allowed to rule as Caesar promised. The Alexandrians were quick to believe this. They were a proud people, made restless by the continued presence in the palace of the powerful Roman. Pothinus' plan began to work. Revolt was in the air.

Pothinus didn't stop there. He saw to it that Caesar's soldiers were given poor food and not much of it. This was not brought to the attention of their commander, and it led to the rise of a mutinous mood among the Romans who wanted to go home.

Even now the scheming Pothinus was not satisfied. He decided that a dead Caesar was the only final solution to his problems. Then and only then would Cleopatra be without the power that protected her. So, with the connivance of Arsinoë and Ganymede, Pothinus laid a plan to have Caesar's wine poisoned.

But Caesar's barber, who heard of the plot when he was not thought to be listening, brought the news to his general. Caesar, with the useful aid of Madrian, confirmed the report. He sent for Pothinus and had him beheaded on the spot.

That, however, did not stop the rising revolt. On the contrary, it added to it. The Alexandrians believed that the real reason for the execution of the high chamberlain lay in his patriotism and his loyalty to Egypt and the King.

Cleopatra and Caesar watched the mobs milling in front of the palace. Even the ships of the Egyptian navy drew away from the harbor, as though to be away from possible action by the ships of Caesar. This was a warlike symptom and Caesar, long experienced in such matters, decided to take some action.

Though he had not wanted to involve Roman troops in any effort to quell the local disturbance, he sent two messengers to Achillas, the commander of the Roman soldiers that were encamped with the Egyptian army outside the city. His message was that the army was to disband, by order of the King and Queen. Achillas was personally to return to Alexandria with his soldiers to aid in putting down the local agitation.

But Achillas now revealed his personal disloyalty to Caesar. Instead of following the instructions brought by the two messengers, he had them slain at once.

Upon hearing this, Ptolemy at once left the palace and joined Achillas and the forces in the desert. He left word that this time, when he returned, he would capture Cleopatra and execute her.

Things were suddenly very hazardous for the Queen and Julius Caesar. The General had brought a good-sized force with him, but many of these soldiers had been allowed home on leave. The Roman troops stationed regularly in Alexandria—on whom Caesar believed he could rely—were with Achillas. Some of Caesar's ships were still in the harbor, but clearly it was impossible for him now to sail away and leave Cleopatra to certain defeat and death.

This battle promised to be a difficult one. Achillas and the army started their move into the city. The beautiful streets became battlefields. Caesar occupied the palace and the surrounding section of the city— also the harbor adjacent to the palace into which his ships now moved. Fortunately this included the great lighthouse, the key to approaches from the sea.

Arsinoë, meanwhile, left the palace with Ganymede. It was not hard for them to steal away. The palace was not well guarded; Caesar needed every man he could lay his hands on to fight as a soldier in the surrounding streets.

As soon as Arsinoë was safely away she proclaimed herself Queen of Egypt. Because of the scheming of Pothinus, Arsinoë had many followers. Ptolemy was away fighting again, so he was not able to defend his throne against this new claim. And Cleopatra had become unpopular in many quarters because of her romance with Caesar which was widely known by now.

But Caesar had enough veteran Roman soldiers and Cleopatra enough devoted troops under General Barak at least to keep the intruding army at bay during the bitter winter. This was a difficult time for the Queen. The old days in the purple tent now seemed easy by comparison. Cleopatra often went out with Caesar, riding beside him on her horse. Some of the time they

lived in a tent just outside the city, but usually they remained in the palace. Cleopatra did everything she could to see that Caesar was comfortable. They were rarely apart. When they were, she was busy planning surprises for him and still trying to find the foods he liked. This was difficult in the midst of war, but love can work miracles and there was no question now that Cleopatra was in love.

One of the worst blows of the winter was struck by Arsinoë and Ganymede. They attempted to cut off the supply of drinking water by running salt sea-water into the pipes that fed the palace area of Alexandria. Caesar met this emergency by taking some men from the fighting line and putting them to work digging new wells.

Perhaps the hardest thing to bear was the destruction of so much beauty in the city. A terrible fire raged through Alexandria. The loss of the treasures in many of its buildings was a loss to the world. Centuries of priceless information about Egypt and the ancient world went up in flame.

Caesar sent many messengers to Rome and other cities, urgently calling for reinforcements. He was still outnumbered and only his vastly superior skill and military sense kept him going.

Not long afterward, Caesar was fighting on land near the Lighthouse of Pharos. Cleopatra with Charmian watched from her window. She had sent Apollodorus with Caesar and it is fortunate that she had.

The Romans decided that they could flank their attackers by taking to small boats. But Caesar's own boat overturned and, dressed in heavy armor, he fell into the chilly, choppy water. Apollodorus, who was in the water with him, helped disengage the armor which would surely have dragged the Roman general down. Then together they swam to a far shore, dodging Egyptian arrows as they went.

Caesar was forced to swim with only one hand because of important papers to which he clung. But, with further assistance from Cleopatra's giant slave, he made the shore safely. He lost only his purple cloak to the enemy because it floated away on the water. Later the Egyptians recovered it. They triumphantly stuck it on a spear and paraded through the city with it.

After that dreadful day, the tide seemed to turn in Caesar's favor. Word came that reinforcements were arriving at last. Fresh Roman legionaries had landed at Pelusium and were making ready to march toward Alexandria. Also, Arsinoë and Ganymede had quarreled with Achillas, a terrible quarrel which ended in the killing of Achillas by Ganymede. Suddenly Arsinoë found herself without a strong military ally, and her backers began to drift away. She was bad-tempered and rude and better able to make enemies than friends. The troops disliked her and soon the fickle Alexandrians were turning on her and blaming her for the destruction in their city.

Caesar decided to leave the palace and the part of the city he had been defending so well. The time had come to take a chance—a big chance. He would appear to move all his troops out of Alexandria and let it be known that he was going to move eastward by land. But in the night he extinguished all the lights on his ships and, guided by the Light of Pharos, sailed westward to join the relief column that was ready to move from Pelusium. Then suddenly and with startling speed he entirely surrounded the forces of Ptolemy, who tried to retreat up the delta of the Nile. The strategy went well for Caesar. By the next day Caesar and his legionaries occupied Ptolemy's own camp.

Frantically trying to escape, the Egyptian army was cut apart. Ptolemy himself, fighting bravely as the end came, fell into the Nile and was drowned. When his body was recovered, Caesar sent to Cleopatra her brother's armor as proof that her enemy and rival was dead.

Caesar then gave orders that Arsinoë be captured and brought to him as a prisoner. He also ordered Ganymede's execution. But before that could be put into effect, Arsinoë's hapless tutor killed himself by falling on a sword.

The Alexandrian war was over. It had lasted for five months. To many people living in other parts of the world in the year 47 B.C. this was just another name to add to the list of Julius Caesar's victories. To the Egyptians, it was the worst defeat they had ever suffered. To the Alexandrians, the loss of the city's treasures as well as the loss of many of their sons and fathers in cruel civil war was almost un- bearable.

For Cleopatra, the war brought an end at last to the Ptolemaic feud that had threatened her crown. It was convincing proof as well of her own conquest of Caesar.

For Julius Caesar, it was the only war that he had ever fought for love. The others had been for glory— the glory of Rome and the glory of Caesar.

In all recorded history only two famous wars have

been waged for a woman. One is the Trojan War, which was fought for beautiful Helen of Troy. The other is the Alexandrian War, waged for Cleopatra of Egypt.

CHAPTER IX

Two Journeys

Alexandria was in a state of great anxiety when Caesar and his legions came marching through the ruined streets. The Alexandrians knew what happened to other cities conquered by the Romans. They were too fearful even to beg for mercy. Sad and silent, they waited, dressed in clothes of mourning as they watched the powerful-looking troops go past.

But Caesar quickly put an end to their fears. He declared that the destruction left by the winter of war was worse than any punishment that he could devise. There would be no further penalty. It was up to them, he said, to rebuild Alexandria into the place of wonder that it had been. He ended his speech by reminding them that the winter was over. It was spring again, the time of rebirth.

Caesar was lenient with the Alexandrians for two reasons. One was his lifelong admiration for Alexander. He wished the city that Alexander had founded to rise again. Second, and even more important, Caesar wanted the capital of Cleopatra's realm to be peaceful.

The next day Caesar publicly restored a radiant Cleopatra to her throne. Soon after, in accordance

with the Ptolemaic tradition, it was arranged that
Cleopatra would now marry her youngest brother. It
was only a marriage of state, called for by the ancient
law laid down by the first Ptolemy. Her brother was
eleven years old, a good-looking, friendly boy. Already
King of Cyprus by decree of Caesar, he would now
be known as Ptolemy XIV. He was the only one in
her family that Cleopatra had any affection for. Caesar
also liked him and gave him his personal horse as a
present.

So far the boy had shown none of the Ptolemaic
greed for power, but Cleopatra arranged that Apollodorus was always to be with him. Now that her kingdom was secure she would take no chances. It was
also arranged to have him tutored every day by the
court scholars, just as Cleopatra had been.

At this time Caesar wrote his *Bellum Alexandrium,*
a report to the senate and the people of Rome. There
is just one line about Cleopatra in it, the only record
that remains about her written by Caesar. He wrote:
"Caesar restored the Queen Cleopatra because she had
been loyal to him and had always remained with him
at headquarters."

The captured Arsinoë was now shipped to Rome
as Caesar's prisoner. When he returned to Rome she
would be marched through the city after him as one
of the souvenirs of his victory.

This would be a terrible punishment for the proud
girl who had wanted to be queen. Cleopatra would
rather have had her executed, but Caesar would not
hear of it. He knew that would have a bad effect on
the people in Rome. They were not as used to family hatreds and killings as the Egyptians. So Arsinoë

sailed away alive, having failed to achieve any of the things she wanted.

Now that the Alexandrian War was over there was no reason why Caesar could not return to Rome, except for his wish to stay with Cleopatra. They were married in an Egyptian rite. Since Caesar already had a wife in Rome, this marriage would have no legal standing in his own country. In Egypt a man could legally have several wives but in Rome only one. Caesar planned to do something about that when he got back there. But in the meantime he was content in Egypt. He and Cleopatra set out on a voyage along the Nile, a journey of celebration and delight.

Caesar and Cleopatra had a state galley for themselves alone. It was a floating palace, named *Thalemeyos,* which rose fifty-four feet above the water. Each of the several stories was surrounded by open decks. On the top there was a lookout tower. The rooms were elaborately decorated. The dining hall had walls of cedar and was the only room on the ship in the Egyptian style. The others were done in the Grecian manner, which was what Cleopatra liked best. In Caesar's cabin, scenes from the Greek epic poem *The Iliad* were painted on the walls.

The great Roman said that he had never seen or dreamed of such a ship. He was sure that even the Pharaohs of long ago had not known such luxury. There was a little chapel dedicated to Aphrodite on board. At one end of the top deck there was even a tiny, charming garden. The decks were all inlaid with amethysts, peridot and jasper.

Four hundred other vessels sailed or rowed after

the *Thalemeyos*. They carried the slaves, Caesar and
Cleopatra's personal attendants, actors and dancing
girls to entertain. Caesar was especially interested in
peformances of Greek dramas. The cooks were in a
boat to themselves with all their equipment and vast
stores of food.

There were also ships occupied by Caesar's army of
several thousand soldiers. He did not expect any trouble or uprisings on the journey. However, it would be
well to be prepared in case of unpleasant surprises.

But the trip was peaceful and happy. It took several weeks, sailing first along the great delta, then
more than a hundred miles upriver. Every moment
along the historic shores was fascinating to Caesar.
He felt that he was beholding the whole history of
Egypt, for Egypt was really the Nile.

He liked to sit on the top deck with Cleopatra.
They sat beneath linen awnings during the day to
protect them from the strong sun. Caesar saw for
himself how Egypt, having so little rain, was wholly
dependent on the river and its system of canals for
its water supply.

One of the canals he saw had been constructed long
before the Trojan War. That was something else
about Egypt which Caesar found exciting—the nearness of the past. One of the places most interesting
to him was the ruins of the still imposing Temple to
the Sun where Plato had once come to study.

It was the General's wish to visit Memphis, which
was the biggest city in Egypt next to Alexandria.
Later he said that by far the most overwhelming
sights he had beheld were the pyramids, symbols of

the old Pharaohs. Standing in the desert sun beside
Cleopatra, he never tired of studying them. He was
amazed by the technical skill of the early Egyptians.

More than ever did Caesar dislike the idea of returning to Rome. This was his first holiday in many
years. He would like to have continued as far as
Ethiopia, but he realized he was overdue at home and
his soldiers were getting restless.

Finally Caesar and Cleopatra reached the difficult
decision. She summoned the admiral of her fleet and
ordered him to turn and sail back to Alexandria.
There Caesar found many messages and reports from
Rome urging his return. He made immediate preparations to depart. But he also promised the Queen to
return to Alexandria soon.

During the last hours of their being together, Cleopatra made a request. She pleaded with Caesar to
take Madrian with him.

"The little man will be lost in Rome," Caesar protested. "He will just be in our way."

"You won't realize he is there," Cleopatra said,
"but he will watch over you. He will never sleep. He
will guard you every minute of the day for me."

At first Caesar refused. She couldn't be serious, he
said. The idea of the dwarf's being useful as a guard
was ridiculous. But Cleopatra persisted and Caesar, to
please her, agreed.

Madrian was proud that the Queen had chosen him.
He was eager to see Rome, but he knew it would not
compare with Alexandria. The day before they were
to sail, Cleopatra spoke to Madrian alone. She made
him swear by his gods that he would first taste everything before Caesar ate or drank it.

The morning of the following day Caesar at last left Alexandria. Cleopatra with Charmian went to the high flat roof of the palace. She stayed there watching for hours until she could no longer make out the shape of the Roman sails against the bright blue sky.

Caesar remained on deck until he saw Egypt fade in the distance. His eyes never left the palace roof and the straight proud figure waving farewell. When the last of the land had vanished he went below to his cabin. He was leaving behind him a queen restored to her throne and to the affection of her people.

He was also leaving behind a queen who would become the mother of his child.

Part Two

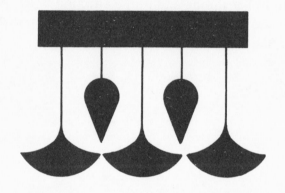

CHAPTER X

Caesarion

A year and a month went by before Caesar and Cleopatra met again. During that time Cleopatra missed Caesar greatly. They had been together almost every day while he was in Egypt.

There was, however, much to keep her busy during the days of Caesar's absence. Alexandria was being rebuilt with amazing speed. The Queen liked to observe the work that was being done. She enjoyed watching the stone masons and other craftsmen at their jobs. She usually made these visits in the afternoon. Charmian and Apollodorus would accompany her. Sometimes Ptolemy, the young king, was allowed to come along as a reward when he had done his lessons well.

But most important of all were preparations for the arrival of Caesar and Cleopatra's child. He was born on June 23rd in the year 47 B.C.—a strong, handsome little boy. There was an unusual air of dignity about his tiny person. He looked out at the world with his father's black eyes. Cleopatra wrote to Caesar that it hardly seemed possible that a newborn baby could look so much like a fully grown man.

From the moment she saw him, Cleopatra adored

her son. She named him Ptolemy Caesar. His name
and the date of his birth were inscribed on the wall
of a temple in Alexandria. In doing this, Cleopatra
followed one of the Egyptians' oldest customs. She
often scorned the old ideas, but she liked this one. It
was right that his birth should be recorded on stone
to carry the event for eternity.

But no one ever called the child Ptolemy Caesar
even though the name was carved in marble. He was
always known as Caesarion, which means little Caesar.

The news of the baby's arrival reached Julius Caesar
when he was far away in Asia Minor. He was overjoyed. At last he had a son. Until the birth of Caesarion
he had had only one child, a daughter, Julia. She
had been an intelligent and lovely girl. Caesar had
adored her, and her early death had been a cruel
blow to him. He was fond of his nephew Octavius
and had decided to adopt him. But now he had a son
of his own. Extra rations of wine were ordered for all
his legions in celebration.

Cleopatra wrote that their son was the healthiest
and happiest baby in all of Egypt. Everyone loved
him. The Alexandrians cheered when he was brought
to the windows of the palace. Apollodorus could carry
him around on just one of his broad hands. Charmian
and Iras spent their days admiring him. His uncle,
Ptolemy, was especially fond of him. The young king
was proud that he could always make the baby laugh.

Egypt was now peaceful, prosperous and free from
the threat of Roman aggression. The Egyptians knew
that this was because of Caesar's high regard for Cleopatra. No queen could have been more popular with
her own people.

While everything was so pleasant in Alexandria, Caesar was on a long, important journey in the East. It was not a peaceful one. First he had gone to the Hellespont, north of the Aegean Sea. There he had had a brief, brisk naval battle with one of Pompey's former generals, Lucius Cassius. Caesar defeated him and then went farther on into Asia Minor. There had been trouble in Pontus, a Roman province beyond Syria. A chieftain, Pharnaces by name and son of the more famous Mithridates, had become powerful enough to rise against Roman dominion. He was resolved to free his people. Caesar was equally determined that he would not. That Rome must rule the world was Caesar's creed.

Caesar had only three legions with him, about 18,000 men. Nevertheless, he marched against Pharnaces and all his men, more than twice the number of his own. At the town of Zela he completely routed them.

After the battle, he sat in his tent and composed a message to the Roman senate, as was his custom. He used just three Latin words: *"Veni, vidi, vici."* ("I came, I saw, I conquered.") This brief dispatch reveals the man just as he must have been.

Caesar then proceeded on the long way back home to Rome, more confident than ever of the reception that awaited him. He landed there in August, approximately two years after his last visit. The welcome he was given outdid anything that Rome had ever known.

Soon after Caesar's arrival, plans were begun for great triumphal processions in which he would ride through the city. He looked forward to this public tribute. But he wanted Cleopatra to see him acclaimed

in this hour of glory. Also, he missed her. So he
wrote that she must come to him as soon as possible.

On the banks of the River Tiber, he prepared for
her a quiet and handsome villa. The gardens adjoined
his own. Although there was much for him to do in
Rome, he took time to arrange for artists and craftsmen to beautify the house and enlarge the gardens.
He ordered hundreds of new trees to be planted to
insure privacy for Cleopatra and their child.

When his invitation arrived in Alexandria, the
Queen was delighted. She had always dreamed of seeing the lands across the sea. But, best of all, she
would be with Caesar again.

It was also arranged by Caesar for Cleopatra and
Ptolemy to be invited officially to Rome for a visit of
state. The purpose of that was to conclude formally
a pact of peace and alliance with the senate.

Cleopatra looked forward to arriving as an honored
guest of the Republic. She thought of her father going to Rome to beg for favors and having to bribe
his way to obtain them. How different would be the
circumstances of her own trip.

When it was announced that the Queen of Egypt
would soon be arriving in Rome, there was much
talk. The Romans were tremendous gossips. Now they
had something to gossip about. There had been many
rumors that the great Caesar was in love with the
Queen of the Nile. Naturally among his friends and
his enemies there was much curiosity to see this almost mythical young woman.

The Romans firmly believed that everyone in the
world except the Greeks and themselves were barbarians. They regarded the Egyptians as particularly

uncivilized because they worshiped gods with the shape of animals: rams, dogs, cats and lion-bodied creatures with strange, smiling faces. Surely the queen of such savages would be a savage herself.

Then finally the day came when Cleopatra, looking from her palace window, saw a large and graceful ship in the harbor. It was an Egyptian vessel with purple sails that had been specially prepared for the voyage across the Mediterranean. In the morning she would be leaving Alexandria at last. Already the men had begun to load the ship that would take her to Rome.

With her, Cleopatra would be carrying to Caesar their child, Caesarion.

CHAPTER XI

The Purple Sails

The morning of the day of departure was clear and bright as the Queen had hoped. She regarded the fine skies as a good omen for the long journey ahead.

Cleopatra was not one who traveled light. The ship's hold bulged with her possessions. Among other things she took with her masses of Egyptian roses, her favorite flower. The entire ship was scented with roses—rich, dark red roses. The Alexandrians had discovered a method of keeping flowers fresh for months. Like many of their secrets, this one was lost, never to be found again.

The cargo also included many presents for Caesar. Some were official gifts—from the Queen of Egypt to the Dictator of Rome. But there were countless personal tokens as well.

The ship was also well filled with people. Many members of her court were with her, among them Charmian, Iras and the strong Apollodorus. They were happy and excited about the trip. Only King Ptolemy, now twelve years old, was a bit sad at leaving Alexandria. He did not share his sister's eagerness to see other countries. He loved Egypt and feared he would be homesick.

The royal baby, Caesarion, was of course too little to know that he was going away. He slept through most of the commotion of the departure.

Cleopatra remembered that her father had always complained bitterly about the Roman food. So she included three skilled cooks in the ship's company as well as big supplies of the wonderful spices and condiments from the markets of Alexandria.

She had also invited several learned men to come with her. One of these was Sosigenes, a celebrated Greek scholar who had originally come to Alexandria to study at the great library. Caesar had met and liked Sosigenes. It was Cleopatra's idea that he might be useful to Caesar. So he came on board the ship as one of Ptolemy's tutors.

Now, at last, she walked slowly down the wide, white steps that led directly from the palace to the inner harbor. The ship was moored at the royal dock. Its sails were still furled tightly to the masts.

The people of the city, by the thousands, lined the rooftops, the wharves and the jetties to say good-by to their Queen-Goddess. When she was on board the signal was given. The ship cast off. The purple sails suddenly unfurled and billowed briskly against the southerly breeze. They were under way.

The vast crowd along the shore started to shout:

"Hail to the Divine Queen!"

"Hail, Cleopatra, daughter of all the gods!"

Cleopatra went to the topmost deck, where she took Caesarion from Iras. He was still asleep and unaware of the excitement of the leave-taking. But as his mother took him, he woke up and smiled at her. She held him high so that he might look at Egypt, the

land of his birth, the land he would one day rule.

But his attention was caught by the flapping and billowing of the great stretches of canvas above his head. He reached out his tiny hands to touch them. This amused Cleopatra, who kissed his cheek, wrapped his blanket closer about him and returned him to Iras.

"Put him to bed in his cabin, Iras."

"Will you not also rest, Divinity?"

"In a little while," Cleopatra replied. "I wish to be here by myself. See that I am not disturbed."

Iras bowed and left. She walked carefully for now the ship was starting to roll, and she carried a precious burden.

Cleopatra watched the coastline of her kingdom get smaller and smaller in the distance. "When will I see Egypt again?" she said softly to herself.

She thought of the many times she had been left behind watching ships sail away and out of sight. This time she was on the ship and her spirit soared. She was on her way to meet the master of the world.

The wind increased, now that the ship was well offshore sailing through deep blue water. The sails strained, the stout timbers creaked as the ship rose and fell with the rolling sea. The salt spray blew against her face and into her hair. She breathed deeply, enjoying it. Charmian appeared noiselessly and wrapped the Queen in a long purple cloak.

Cleopatra continued to stay there until she could no longer see land. "Good-by," she called aloud. "Good-by, my country!"

For her it was a moment of destiny. Tonight her astrologer would tell her that never before had her star been so high in the heavens.

CHAPTER XII

Hail Caesar!

Cleopatra's arrival in Rome was celebrated with all the splendor and pomp that Caesar could command. He was waiting for her at the gates of the city when she arrived from Rome's seaport of Ostia. With him were many members of the senate and other high officials. There were several speeches of welcome. The Queen responded to these in a manner that won compliments.

Then Caesar escorted her to a large chariot. Standing beside it was little Madrian, dressed in full Roman armor and as full of excitement and self-importance as ever. He fell at the Queen's feet in a frenzy of affection, and she was overjoyed to see him again.

Cleopatra drove slowly through the city of Rome with her brother sitting beside her. The streets were packed with people eager for a glimpse of the foreign rulers. Expecting this, Cleopatra had put on an elaborate dress of silver cloth and many strings of pearls. Pearls were entwined in her hair. Caesar thought she looked more beautiful and regal than he had remembered. How unlike the young girl who had risen from the carpet that night at the palace!

The Romans were dazzled by her appearance. She returned their frank stares kindly and with interest. She did not smile. It was too soon to smile, she thought. She would wait to be sure that they were well disposed toward her and her son.

Cleopatra was astonished by the appearance of the city. It was dirty and congested. Most of the streets were extremely narrow and crooked. Some were paved

with heavy cobblestones to take the traffic of chariots and cavalry. Everywhere there seemed to be confusion and noise. Nowhere did she see the beauty and order that she was used to in Alexandria.

Her chariot turned at the end of a twisting street, and the Queen beheld before her for the first time the brown waters of the Tiber.

"So this is the great Roman river," she whispered

to her brother. "The Nile could easily swallow it!"

They crossed over a bridge, starting to leave the city behind. In a short time they drew up before a large villa. Romans considered this villa to be magnificent. Actually it could not compare with the luxury and beauty of the royal palace at Alexandria. But Cleopatra was delighted. Caesar had done everything to make things comfortable for her. The gardens were the wonder of Rome. There was a lovely park of pines and ilex trees which Caesar himself had designed. Here, he and the Queen could walk unseen and undisturbed.

Inside, the house had been redecorated for her in a lavish way. There were deep chairs and divans. Priceless rugs were spread on the floors. There were many silken pillows, for Cleopatra loved to have pillows everywhere. Soft curtains were hung for privacy.

Cleopatra exclaimed with pleasure at every evidence of Caesar's attention to details she might care for. Outside her bedroom was a small walled garden for her private use. She also had a superb bathroom with a sunken tub, almost a pool, of purplish-red Egyptian porphyry. The Romans were far advanced in their plumbing; an excellent system of pipes brought both hot and cold water into their best houses.

After Caesar had shown her about, they went together into the garden. It was wonderfully quiet after the turmoil of her arrival. They sat together for a while on a marble bench that was placed in the shade of a large and ancient tree. Caesarion was brought to them and laughed and played for a while in the grass at their feet. Caesar was entranced now at last to hold in his own arms the son he had wished for.

A week after the Queen's arrival there took place
the first of four great triumphs in Caesar's honor.
These were processions in the Roman tradition cele-
brating great military victories. No one but Julius
Caesar had ever had so many as four.

The night before they began, Caesar came across
the Tiber to have dinner alone with Cleopatra. He
brought with him a delicate and lovely coronet of
gold and precious stones. He found her waiting for
him on a low couch in her favorite room on the second floor of the villa. He showed her what he had
brought, then placed it on her dark curls.

"If you will wear it publicly tomorrow it would
please me," he said.

"That is not a difficult favor to grant," she replied,
laughing.

"You have many crowns," said Caesar.

"None that you have given me," said the Queen.
"That makes this the one I care for most."

"It will not be the last I shall give you." Caesar
spoke in a voice suddenly serious.

Cleopatra caught her breath. During the week that
she had been in Rome, she had put out of her mind
all thoughts of her own ambition. But now she suddenly felt the Ptolemaic love of power. Between them,
she and Caesar could rule the world and leave that
world to their son.

They talked no more of crowns or kingdoms that
evening, but nothing could stop Cleopatra from thinking about them.

The next morning she was driven into Rome. From
the top of one of its seven hills, she could see
for the first time some of the more noble buildings of

the city—the senate, the forum, the temples and the sacred shrine of the vestal virgins.

Cleopatra was completely rested from her long journey. She wore one of her flowing robes in white, and over her shoulders a long cloak of royal purple. On her head rested the delicate crown that Caesar had given her the night before. About her arms were the heavy bracelets worn by all Egyptian queens at great functions. She was shining with pride in Caesar, in herself and in their child.

She was well seated in a special box prepared for her and her attendants on the tribune where sat the entire senate and high officials of the republic. The triumphal procession would pass directly in front of them and then wind its way throughout the city.

Suddenly trumpets were heard, followed by the rolling roar of drums. A massed phalanx of armored soldiers, one man from every legion in the army, now passed, carrying the *fasces* and other symbols of the power of Rome. These were followed by a procession of sixty maidens, with garlands in their hair, throwing flower petals onto the ground. Off to one side, a cavalry band of a hundred mounted musicians, including bagpipers, filled the air with a stirring march of victory.

Then, in the bright sunlight, Julius Caesar appeared through an archway built especially for the occasion. He was standing in a carved and decorated chariot, drawn by four perfectly matched spirited horses. As he advanced, the great conquerer raised one arm high in the Roman salute. The immense crowd roared its admiration. As if with one voice they cried, "Hail Caesar! . . . Hail Caesar!"

Caesar's black eyes scanned the tribune, seeking Cleopatra.

At just the moment he saw her, something happened to the chariot. He stumbled. It seemed as though he would surely fall. But quickly he regained his balance and leaped from the chariot.

The spectators gasped with relief. A near tragedy had been averted. But what had gone wrong? The answer was simple. An axle had broken. At once another chariot was wheeled into position, and the procession started up again as if nothing had happened.

To the Queen it had been a moment of horror. She was highly superstitious. In Egypt Caesar had often teased her about finding omens and portents in everything. The broken axle, which seemed merely an annoyance to everyone else, was a true warning of evil to Cleopatra. For the first time since leaving Alexandria she felt fear.

Being Cleopatra, she did not show her fear to anyone. Inwardly she was trembling. But the smile that she gave to Caesar as he passed, and the face that she presented to the Romans all about her was as bright as the morning.

After Caesar passed, and as the procession of troops and hostages continued, every eye turned occasionally to look at the Egyptian queen. Everyone in the city now knew the reason for her being there. And much as they adored Caesar, there was plenty of grumbling against what the people regarded as an alien intrusion into a great Roman celebration.

The highborn ladies of Rome also resented her presence among them. After all, they said, although Caesar might have married Cleopatra under Egyptian law, he was not married to her under Roman law. Behind all this may have been the force of jealousy against the beautiful stranger. But also it expressed the high regard of the Romans—at that time—for strict legal and moral standards.

Several days later came the second triumph. This one was to celebrate Caesar's victory in the Alexandrian War. It was an especially important day for Cleopatra. It showed all the Roman people that she was the rightful and lawful ruler of Egypt. It proved to the senate how unwise they had been to favor her defeated and dead brother.

Large pictures of Pothinus and Achillas, her former enemies, were this time carried in front of Caesar's chariot. She looked at them with pleasure. It was all she could do not to laugh out loud.

In the midst of music and cheering, Caesar passed, attired this time in armor of solid gold. It seemed to Cleopatra that he was surely the most impressive man alive.

Then, suddenly, following behind Caesar's chariot, came something for which Cleopatra was completely unprepared. It was her sister Arsinoë, walking slowly and in chains, a prisoner of war.

Cleopatra stared at the terrible spectacle. Arsinoë's dress was ragged and torn. Her hair was dirty and uncombed. She had no shoes on her feet, and her chains bound both her wrists and her ankles. She trudged along behind her captor, her head downcast. She was the picture of utter misery and despair.

There was a gasp of horror from some of the more sympathetic Romans. Many looked at the Queen to see how she felt at this sight of her degraded sister.

But Cleopatra betrayed no emotion. She just held her little turquoise perfume bottle to her nose.

After Arsinoë, there followed a dozen bewildered giraffes. They were another trophy in the show. The crowds forgot about Arsinoë in their excitement at seeing these exotic animals.

Cleopatra did not look at them. Her eyes followed Arsinoë as she moved pitifully away—Arsinoë, who had dared to try to be queen. Cleopatra's red lips curved in contempt.

She never forgot that sight of her sister. She never forgot the sound of the screaming crowd. She knew now what happened to anyone brought as a defeated hostage to Rome. She remembered that to the end of her life. It was to have an enormous influence on her some years later.

But on that sunny morning of the second triumph she rejoiced in Arsinoë's defeat and in her own good fortune.

CHAPTER XIII

Octavius

As the weeks passed happily, Cleopatra was asked by Caesar to pose for a full-figure statue of herself. He did not tell her what it was for, but it was executed by one of the foremost sculptors in Rome.

Soon after the statue was completed, the Queen learned why he wished it. Her surprise was shared by all of Rome. Caesar, who was believed to be an actual descendant of Venus, the goddess of love, had built a new temple to give thanks to her for his victories.

He invited everyone of importance in the city to attend the dedication of the shrine and made the day an official holiday. Even the schools were closed. There were public feasts and spectacles to entertain the crowd. Elephants and apes which had been brought by Caesar from Africa were displayed. At night comedies and dramas were performed.

Everyone had to agree that the new temple to Venus was one of the most beautiful buildings in Rome. But the thing about it that created the greatest excitement was the lovely statue in the forecourt that represented the goddess.

It was the figure of Cleopatra!

Caesar had also ordered new coins to be minted. They bore on one side an image of Cleopatra as Venus and on the other a tiny portrait of Caesarion as Cupid, child of the goddess.

Some Roman citizens were merely amused at this fresh evidence of the Dictator's devotion to the "Egyptian," as they called her. Many more were shocked and offended. But neither opinion mattered in the least to Caesar.

It was natural on this great occasion that the Dictator should be surrounded by all his relations. Romans, more than anybody, had great pride in their family connections. This was especially true of so patrician a line as Caesar's.

Cleopatra now met them all. But the one upon whom her attention fastened itself was a young man to whom she took an instant dislike. He seemed about seventeen years old. His complexion was pale to the point of being sallow, and he was very thin. But he was tall and his eyes shone almost as if he had a fever. His name was Octavius, and he was Caesar's grandnephew, the grandson of his sister Julia.

The Queen attempted to talk to him pleasantly. She asked him questions and tried to draw him out. He answered reluctantly. He was clearly ill at ease. No doubt he felt the natural hostility between them. There was plenty of reason for it to exist.

Several years before, the father of Octavius had died. Caesar, who liked the boy, had recently made him an adopted son. This was quite a common Roman practice. Also it was generally expected that he would be Caesar's heir.

It is certain that Octavius himself expected this. His position was a legal one. No other legal heir was in sight, and there was not likely to be one unless Caesar did something about Caesarion.

This rivalry was certainly in the mind of both Cleopatra and Octavius when they met. The young man had been brought to her villa by Caesar, but left soon after a meeting which was not very successful.

Caesar sensed that Cleopatra had not cared for Octavius, but he did not pursue the subject. For one thing, Octavius was of his family. Family loyalty was a Roman obligation. Also, the boy was his adopted son. It was not fitting even for Cleopatra to reflect upon his merits.

Nevertheless, Caesar realized that he must soon have Caesarion accepted as his actual son and heir. To achieve this he would have to make legal his marriage to Cleopatra. Under existing Roman law this would be impossible, and a change in the law would be difficult to accomplish, even with all his power. There was great dislike in Rome for the oriental custom of a man's having more than one wife. But he would start to use his great influence in the senate to start a movement toward this change.

With his feeling for close family ties, Caesar brought Octavius back several times to see the Queen. He hoped that if he brought them together frequently, Cleopatra would learn to like the lad.

But no warmth developed between them. On the contrary, Cleopatra made certain that whenever Octavius came, he was not allowed to see the little Caesarion. She did not want them to be alone for an instant. Her training and long breeding as a Ptolemy showed itself in her behavior. Hers was a family where hate and murder were the rule, and she would take no chances with the life of her son.

Meanwhile a popular feeling surged through Rome that Caesar should be finally crowned as absolute monarch. He refused to agree to this, wanting more proof that such a desire was shared by all. But destiny was pressing him on.

To Cleopatra it seemed that it would surely be only a short time before Caesar was made king, and their son named heir to his throne. But in the long hours of the chilly Roman nights, her thoughts often turned to Octavius. Her instincts warned her well, for the day was to come when Octavius would bring great trouble.

CHAPTER XIV

Friends and Romans

It was a strange new world in which Cleopatra now found herself. Everything was different from her life in Alexandria—the climate, the food and, above all, the people.

Roman society was very curious about her. There had been speculation about what she would do and how she would behave. They could scarcely believe that she would live so quietly. In fact, they were rather disappointed that the Queen of Egypt did not give great parties in the colorful oriental style they had heard about.

Cleopatra would have done anything that Caesar wanted, but he was bored with banquets and with many of the Romans. For two years she saw no one without his approval. However, she saw many who were useful to the Dictator or amused him. Her policy of seclusion caused resentment among Romans of importance who were not invited to Cleopatra's house. They blamed her and began to spread false and scandalous stories about her.

But the rumors didn't bother the Queen. She even laughed at some of the more outrageous ones. She was too happy to care what people said. She was re-united with Caesar, whom she loved devotedly.

During all this time, Caesar was extremely busy with matters of state. He now held three positions of high importance. He was Dictator, First Consul and Pontifex Maximus. The last was his title as a supreme religious leader. It also gave him absolute protection, under Roman law, against attack. Violence against his person in any form would be an unthinkable crime.

This was an important protection for a man in Caesar's position. Rome, even under his rule, was alive with politics and trouble. Conflicting parties and groups frequently turned to the murder of those with whom they disagreed. As Pontifex Maximus, Caesar was now beyond any such risk. At least so everyone thought.

Many of his problems and plans he brought to Cleopatra, whose intelligence and skill as a ruler he much respected. During the two years she was in Rome great improvements were started for the welfare of the people. Rents and taxes were reduced, and Roman laws made more equal for all.

Caesar encouraged the development of towns all over Italy, with strong ties to Rome as their leader. He urged the people of the city, which was very crowded, to colonize the places he had conquered. He wanted to bring Roman ideas and law to those remote places. As a result, many Roman communities began to flourish throughout the lands we know today as France, Spain, England and the Middle East.

To accomplish all this, as well as many other proj-ects and plans, Caesar needed the support of the sen-ate and other Roman leaders. So Cleopatra's quiet

villa across the Tiber became a center for the most in-
fluential and interesting men in Rome. There Caesar
could relax with them and at the same time make
good political progress.

Among those who came was Caesar's old friend, a
most important Roman named Marcus Brutus. During
Caesar's bitter civil war with Pompey, Brutus had
taken Pompey's side and even fought in the field for
him. But because Caesar admired him so greatly and
because of their former friendship, his life was spared
after the defeat of Pompey at Pharsalus. More recently, as a token of further forgiveness, Caesar had
made Brutus one of the governors of Gaul.

When Caesar had first related this to Cleopatra she
had been shocked. "How can you spare the life of a
friend who has been treacherous?" she asked.

"Brutus has great ability," said Caesar. "He is not
a soldier but a man of unusual intellect. Rome needs
him. So do I. It would have been wasteful to kill a
man of his experience."

"But he was against you."

Caesar looked at her patiently. "Brutus chose Pompey because he felt it was the right thing to do. He
is a man of high principle."

The Queen thought about this for a moment. To a
woman of the Ptolemaic blood it was absurd ever to
trust a traitor. "He may think of principles but not of
people," she said. "He is a cold man."

There was another man whom Cleopatra did not
like. Nor did Caesar like him either. But they put up
with him not only because he had grown to importance but also because he was the brother-in-law of
Brutus. His name was Gaius Cassius. Cassius had an

irritating manner; he was sly and secretive. But he was also competent and clever. Caesar, who was above all things a remarkably fair man, set aside his personal dislike and invited Cassius often to the villa. More than that, he made him a *praetor* of Rome. This charged him with the administration of justice.

Cleopatra concealed her dislike for these two important men so well that they both were fascinated by her. Brutus enjoyed talking to the Queen about the Greek philosophers, the leading thinkers of their day. He could quote them from memory; so could Cleopatra.

Brutus, she realized, was a man of influence as well as taste and learning. She could understand his hold on Caesar. But to her, Cassius seemed a greedy man —greedy for both money and power.

Then one night, rather unexpectedly, a rare and remarkable guest came to the villa. His name was Cicero. Although he was a great political figure in Rome, he lived in semiretirement. But his influence as an orator was enormous.

Cicero had also sided with Pompey against Caesar. But Caesar, again with his capacity for forgiveness, admired Cicero's gifts as an orator and invited him to meet the Queen of Egypt. Perhaps Caesar felt that the charms of Cleopatra would warm Cicero up a bit to his side. But instead there was an immediate hostility between them. In a letter to a friend Cicero wrote, "I detest Cleopatra. She is insolent and gives me no credit for spirit or feelings."

Hearing of this, Cleopatra said to Caesar, "How can I give him credit for what he doesn't have?"

He said nothing.

"Sometimes I cannot understand you," she went on.

"Cicero talks against you and the people are listening to him."

"Let them listen. I would not stop them if I could."

She laughed. In all the world was there such a man!

One person presented himself to the Queen without Caesar's permission. This was an elderly man named Ammonius, a Levantine, who came originally from the far eastern shores of the Mediterranean. Now he was a Roman citizen, a banker, and very rich. He had been a friend of Cleopatra's father when Ptolemy Auletes was in Rome and had loaned the Egyptian ruler large sums of money. Cleopatra was pleased to see Ammonius—not only because of his services to her father, but also because he was a most amusing talker and a great gossip.

Among other things, she was able to find out from him something that had puzzled her. She had wondered why among all those friends of Caesar's brought by him to the villa he had never included the popular Mark Antony. Some instinct had kept her from asking the reason, until the visit of Ammonius gave her the chance.

Cleopatra learned that when Caesar returned from Egypt he had found Mark Antony deeply in debt. This was the result of wild living and extravagance that were the scandal of Rome. Only his good looks and gaiety had protected him against complete disapproval by all official and social Rome.

When Antony came to welcome and congratulate his old friend, he was met by a dictator who disliked heartily what he had heard. Antony tried to defend himself but couldn't. The record of his behavior was clear. Caesar was outraged that a man of Antony's great ability and promise should so degrade himself.

But Antony had a high temper and would take no criticism. Apparently the two men quarreled and Caesar told Antony he had no wish to see him again. In fact, he even suggested that Antony should leave Rome for a while until his public reputation had improved a bit. This Antony did the following day, taking with him a notorious actress as his companion.

Caesar was saddened by this occurrence. He knew of Antony's personal loyalty to him and admired immensely his courage as a soldier.

To Cleopatra, also, this was an unhappy state of affairs. She had looked forward to seeing again the brave and handsome cavalry officer she had met as a child.

Perhaps the most exciting of all the things being discussed at the villa was Caesar's plan to set up an entirely new calendar to mark the period of the weeks and months. He felt that the old Roman calendar was clumsy and impractical. It was based on the twenty-eight-day cycle of the moon. This didn't work too well as there were always days left over in the computation of the year.

To end the confusion once and for all, Caesar put to work the Greek scientist Sosigenes, whom Cleopatra had brought from Alexandria as a tutor for young Ptolemy. He assigned to him a number of Roman astronomers with instructions that they devise a new arrangement for the division of the year. They finally figured out the calendar of 365 days with a day added every four years.

This calendar is the one still used today. It was called the Julian calendar in Julius Caesar's honor. As a further tribute, his name was given to one of the months— July, which had been the time of his triumphs.

Astronomy and the stars had always meant a great deal to the Egyptians. So Cleopatra was especially delighted by this work. Her villa was filled with astronomers' charts and drawings of the sky and remarkable devices for the telling of time. Young Ptolemy, who lived in a house of his own near by, shared his sister's interest.

Winter had now come to Rome, Cleopatra's first winter in a foreign land. The rain fell on bare trees and empty flower beds. A chilly wind blew through the valleys and up the river. It made a sad, sighing sound around the house.

Cleopatra's thoughts turned to Egypt. The sun would be shining there, large and yellow as honey. Only soft breezes would stir the sweet-smelling air. For the first time, the Queen of the Nile began to miss her country.

CHAPTER XV

Difficult Days

That winter was the coldest Rome had known in years. Cleopatra wondered if she would ever be warm again. She wore thick woolen cloaks over her thin Egyptian dresses, and Caesar sent her blankets of fur. Small braziers of burning coals were placed all over the house in an effort to produce some heat.

Then illness followed. First it was young King Ptolemy who awakened one morning with a chill. His bones trembled with the dampness rising from the Tiber. The best doctors in Rome were hurried to his bedside, and because he was young and strong he soon recovered.

During the days when he still had to stay in bed, Cleopatra would read to him about Egypt. They would both wonder how things were progressing there. What new buildings had been erected? What ships were in the harbor? They talked as people do who love and miss their homeland.

Then the Queen herself fell ill. She had gone to dine at the house of a well-to-do senator named Rufus, which was near hers. There she had eaten a thickish, pasty dish which she enjoyed. She had never had it anywhere before, and probably she ate too much of it. Today a somewhat refined version of that same dish is called spaghetti.

Only little Caesarion appeared to be completely able to take anything that Rome had to offer in the way of food or weather. His health was perfect. Caesar was proud of his little son.

"You see," he said, "he is a true Roman. He will be a good soldier."

"He is your son," replied Cleopatra. "He will be good at whatever he does!"

During these days, Caesar was not seen often at the villa. The confusions in Rome were mounting. One of the worst things he had to deal with was a mutiny by some soldiers of the returned legions. Thousands of them rioted through the streets of Rome, burning and even killing.

The mutiny was caused by some of their leaders who were old veterans. They felt they were not receiving fair treatment at their time of discharge. As a result, there was panic in the city, and it took Caesar quite some time to get the situation under control, despite his influence with the troops.

Then, just as Caesar and Cleopatra were making plans to go to the south of Italy in quest of some sun and warmth, a rebellion suddenly broke out in the Roman province of Spain. At first, it seemed to be a simple uprising such as Rome had to deal with all the time. But then the leaders of the rebellion turned out to be the two sons of Pompey, Caesar's defeated and dead rival. They were urging insurrection against Rome, and their appeal found response all over Spain. What had started as a small local fight for the Roman garrison was taking on the look of a war. If the Pompeys were not defeated, Rome would lose the vast province of Spain.

Cleopatra was not surprised when she learned that Caesar must leave for the front. For his sake she suppressed her deep feeling of disappointment and tried to play the role of a Roman wife.

"I know that where the fighting is thickest you will be," she said. "Promise me you will take care."

He promised, but it was a promise he did not keep. Later, after his return, he was to say, "Usually I fight for victory. In Spain I was fighting for my life."

It was a brief but bloody war. The Pompeys had succeeded in gathering a large army of young men. They were not trained, but they were brave and eager. Against them Caesar led a much smaller army, but his men were veterans.

In the end, it was the genius of the commanding general that brought the victory. Caesar outwitted and outplayed his enemies. Not content with that, he went into combat with drawn sword again and again to encourage his exhausted soldiers.

While these terrible events were going on in Spain, Cleopatra filled her loneliness by working for Caesar's cause in Rome. She learned that Cicero had written a letter to Caesar which he was showing to everyone in Rome. Actually, she soon found out that Cicero had not dared to send the letter to Caesar himself. When she obtained a copy of it she could understand why.

The letter started off by telling Caesar that, if he won the war in Spain, he would return to Rome as great a conquerer as Alexander had been. But Cicero went on to say that he hoped Caesar would also be like Alexander in his refusal ever to be crowned a king. This was Cicero's way of dealing with the report that Caesar might assume the royal rank and title.

Copies of the letter had been made and distributed all over Rome. Cicero's views had great influence with Romans of all classes. Also, final word of the result of the battle in Spain had not yet been received. People felt that overpraising Caesar might give Rome further trouble with the sons of Pompey if they were not completely defeated.

Madrian brought the Queen constant information about groups that were meeting secretly to act against Caesar's growing power. They felt that if he returned victorious he would demand even more. That much power could, even with so exceptional a man as Caesar, turn him into a tyrant.

From her friend Ammonius, she learned that similar meetings had been held at the home of Cassius. Brutus had been there on some of those occasions. This did not surprise the Queen.

She wrote frequently to Caesar but heard rarely from him. His military progress was swift and the mails between them difficult. She gave him indications of the plottings in Rome, so that he could deal with them as he wished. His few letters to her gave a wonderful account of what was happening. He was a fine writer, especially about warfare.

Few of the reports from him were encouraging. The conditions for fighting were the worst he had ever encountered. The weather was bitter cold; the mountain roads, narrow and dangerous. His enemies were young and very brave. Between the lines, she knew that he was telling her that he was no longer a boy.

One thing the Queen did not enjoy hearing was that Caesar's adopted son, Octavius, was fighting as an officer by his side. Caesar stated that the boy was valiant and showed ability as a leader. It was the first time Octavius had been involved in military action.

Caesar also reported that one of the enemy leaders was Titus Libernius, who had once been a trusted lieutenant on the staff of Caesar. He knew many of the great general's tricks of strategy and was now using them against him. As a result, Caesar had to invent completely different tactics from those he had often relied on in the past.

Then came a day at a small town called Munda, near Seville. Things had gone badly. Caesar's men were weary. Defeat was in the air. The sun was setting. The enemy's army, full of confidence, had settled down for the night.

Suddenly and unbelievably, a mass frontal attack by Caesar's troops began in full force. The Pompey elements, unformed and unready, were thrown off balance. Leading his men personally into the thickest of the fighting was Caesar himself. Up and down the line he called to them, "Come, my men from many battles! Are we to be defeated by boys who never won a war?"

The surprise of the attack, and perhaps the grim desire of Caesar's soldiers to finish the conflict, carried the battle. When the Pompey troops started to stampede, breaking into sections, the skilled legionaries mowed them down, unit by unit.

When it was all over, Caesar had killed 30,000 of the enemy and lost only 1,000 himself. It was one of

the greatest victories of his life. The Spanish rebellion was at an end. Now again he could go back to Rome and to Cleopatra.

By the time Caesar returned, so had the spring. The thrilling news of his arrival in the city was brought to Cleopatra by Madrian. She could hardly wait to see him, nor had she long to wait. He came to see her even before he reported to the senate.

Some days later she was expecting him again. She awaited him in the garden and looked at her reflection in a little mirror of polished metal. She wondered if he would like the new way she had arranged her hair.

Hearing his voice, she put the mirror aside and ran like a girl across the lawn. Then she saw him. She also saw that he was not alone.

She stopped and stood quite still. The late afternoon sun was shining in her eyes. It was hard to see who was walking toward her with Caesar. He was a tall man—so tall that Caesar appeared slight beside him. He had broad shoulders, and was burned by the sun.

Cleopatra watched the two coming across the garden. They walked in step and talked earnestly to each other. They had not yet seen her. She was still hidden by the trees.

Caesar said something to his companion that made him laugh. He threw his head back, shouting with laughter, showing his strong, white teeth.

Cleopatra knew that she had heard that laugh before. Now they were close enough so that she could see the man plainly. She stepped out past the screen of trees.

Caesar caught sight of her. She was standing half in sunlight, half in shadow. Her long pleated skirt moved in the soft breeze.

"I have brought an old friend to see you," Caesar said.

For a moment she had been startled. But now she was composed as she stepped forward to greet her visitor.

The tall, bronzed man bent his dark head over her hand. It seemed very small in his large brown hand.

"Your Majesty," he said gravely.

The Queen smiled at him. "It is good to see you again, Mark Antony."

CHAPTER XVI

A Crown for Caesar

They sat down under the trees—Cleopatra, Caesar and Mark Antony—and talked of many things. The two men had not seen each other since the early spring. Now it was nearing summer.

Antony had gone to meet Caesar in Spain. Caesar had been so grateful to see his old friend that they both had quickly forgotten the reasons for their quarrel. The relationship between the two seemed warm and natural. Antony insisted that he well remembered Cleopatra as the little princess in her father's palace. They spoke of her father, whom Antony had helped regain his throne from Berenice. He also remembered well the ugly Berenice.

"You are remarkably unlike your sister, Majesty," he said. His eyes were full of laughter.

Caesar asked for Caesarion. Iras brought him from the house. The boy had just awakened from his nap and he regarded Antony with the bright, black eyes that were so like his father's. Then, suddenly shy, he ran to his mother.

Mark Antony thought that he had rarely seen a

lovelier sight than this slender, beautiful young woman and her rosy little boy. He observed Caesar looking at them both with love and pride.

Antony loved and admired Caesar above all men. He had deeply regretted their quarrel and blamed himself for it. He knew Caesar to be the most just and forgiving of men. Now he was happy to see that his friend had found such happiness, and he was more pleased than ever that their friendship was mended.

As Cleopatra chattered on, it was clear that she was glad Caesar had found again such a loyal and strong friend. Rome was full of treachery. Antony would be needed by them both in the days that lay ahead.

At last Antony rose, as if to leave.

"You must have dinner with us," said Caesar.

"I should greatly like to," replied Antony, as he looked at the Queen.

"Of course you must," she quickly responded.

When they went into the house, Antony praised everything he saw. Cleopatra remembered his enthusiasm from the old days at the palace. Everything had amused and interested him. He had not changed. It was easy to see why he was so well liked. He enjoyed things and people and jokes. The very air was charged with his pleasure. He had such a good time that others caught it from him.

They had an excellent dinner. Antony said that he would have known it was cooked by an Egyptian cook. No Roman had such a talent for food.

Cleopatra could see that he admired the rich comfort of her house. He was especially interested in the things she had brought with her from Egypt, such as the jeweled tripods that held golden bowls of burning incense to perfume the rooms.

"It reminds me of Alexandria," he said, as he sniffed the scented air.

Caesar began talking about the days and nights of the last battle at Munda.

"What would you have done if you had lost that battle?" asked Antony.

Caesar did not hesitate. "I would have killed myself," he replied. "I would never have let them take me prisoner."

Cleopatra shivered at the thought. "What a prize of war you would have been!" she said.

Caesar smiled. "I cannot quite see myself being led as a trophy through the streets of Rome."

Mark Antony became a regular visitor to the villa. He was the handsomest man in Rome, and he had charm and vitality as well. Before many weeks had passed Caesar appointed him as a Second Consul of Rome, a high and powerful office. To everyone's surprise, Antony proved to be hard-working and serious-minded. His days of riotous living appeared to be behind him.

Caesar was pleased by Antony's progress. He had always admired him as a soldier. Now he realized how valuable his friend could be in the political life of the state. In the meantime, Antony was finding every opportunity to impress upon the people of Rome Caesar's right to be their crowned king.

One day in February Caesar was seated on a chair

of state overlooking the great market place. Races and games were taking place in celebration of an important holiday. The place was filled with a huge throng, and Caesar was in the center of it where he could be seen by all. He was dressed in his triumphal robes.

Suddenly Mark Antony advanced toward Caesar in sight of everybody. He offered to him a handsome crown of gold, woven with bay leaves.

"You are our king!" said Antony. "The time has come for you to accept a crown from your people."

There was tremendous excitement at this, many cheering Antony on and others protesting. Caesar rose and put up his arm against receiving the honor.

Twice again Antony and others about him pressed the crown on Caesar, who finally said in a loud voice so that all might hear, "I am Caesar, not king!"

With those words he left the market place, making his way slowly through the screaming thousands.

Antony followed him. That night at Cleopatra's house Caesar was moody and troubled.

"You have seen today that they want you to be king," said Cleopatra.

"I am not so sure of it," replied Caesar. His wisdom and his knowledge of people caused his uncertainty.

"But you already have everything except the title itself. Why not have that as well?" demanded Antony.

Caesar thought for a long moment. Then slowly he said, "Perhaps I have too much already. The gods will provide an answer."

Later that night as he was leaving, Antony had a chance to talk for a moment with Cleopatra alone.

"He must be crowned king—and the time is now," he whispered to her.

"I agree, Mark Antony."

She did agree. But there was a shadow of anxiety over the brightness of her days.

CHAPTER XVII

The Prophecy

All Rome was talking about Caesar's actions. Even his staunchest admirers were confused. He kept saying that he did not want to be named king. Yet each day his behavior grew more regal.

When the statues of the gods were carried in a procession, Caesar's statue was there too. On Capitol Hill next to the seven statues of the ancient Roman kings an eighth appeared. It was a golden statue of Julius Caesar. This was done by his order and everybody knew it.

In the senate hall he had a throne of gold made for himself, in which he sat. He remained seated even while addressing the senate. This created alarm and offense. Rome buzzed with unrest. A large portion of Romans did not want a monarch. They continued to put their trust in a republican form of government. They were frightened by Caesar's conduct. Many citizens still loyal and devoted to him were beginning to feel that he did have too much power. It seemed unwise to them that the destiny of Rome should be in the hands of a single being, even if he was Julius Caesar.

Caesar paid no attention to the rumors which reached him. He was impatient with any block that the senate raised to his many plans and projects. He felt that he knew what was best for his country, and he wanted to act on his convictions at once without bothering about permissions and agreements. Various senators were heard to say that he no longer took the trouble to be tactful to gain his ends. The question most often asked was: "If an individual has absolute authority must it not lead in the end to tyranny?"

Caesar continued to say that he believed in the tradition of the republic. He had believed in it all his life and had fought for it because he believed that it was the best form of government the world had known. All he wished for Rome was freedom and democracy.

The difference of public opinion about him was sharply marked that winter in Rome. Caesar's conquests, as well as his generous and merciful policies, had made him an idol. But to many the idol was being replaced by the threat of a tyrant.

Cleopatra was kept informed about both points of view. Most of what she heard troubled her. She became increasingly nervous and apprehensive.

But if she was nervous, Caesar was not. He listened calmly to the tales of plots and conspiracies against him. Many times Cleopatra herself gave him these reports. He would listen attentively, then proceed exactly as before.

He was busy organizing laws and reforms that would benefit Rome and the colonies. To Cleopatra it seemed that he was continually presenting new decrees to the senate. He discussed almost everything with her. He started work on the seaport of Ostia, near Rome, to enlarge and improve it. New canals were begun. This was a direct result of the excellent canals he had seen in Egypt. Influenced by Alexandria's appearance, he also imposed a system for cleaning the streets of Rome. Previously they had been littered with refuse and were anything but a credit to such a great city. Nothing about Rome, Cleopatra observed, was too large or too small for his attention.

He had said he would draft a bill that would allow him to marry Cleopatra under Roman law, and therefore make Caesarion his legal and political heir. But that bill was lost in the mass of other things. Perhaps he thought it could wait. Perhaps the time did not seem right to press it.

One of the reasons he kept up this driving pace was that he had decided to leave Rome in March. With his legions he was going to Parthia, in Asia Minor. There he intended to make the eastern frontiers more secure. Then he would join Cleopatra in Egypt. After that they would return to Rome together, traveling slowly through eastern Europe. The whole trip would take about two years.

Caesar greatly looked forward to this expedition. He regarded himself as primarily a soldier. He was tired of being a politician. While he was away he would continue his writing about the campaigns he had fought and won. His wish was to leave this personal record behind him.

The Queen was delighted with these plans. For one thing, she would worry less about Caesar when he was away from Rome. Now she sensed danger whenever she looked at an unfriendly face. Also she was as eager as her brother to see her country again. Ptolemy was not well. Cleopatra knew that his first glimpse of Alexandria would cure him.

There would be much for her to do in Egypt. She had been away for two years. The time would pass quickly until Caesar joined her.

She was glad that Caesarion, now three years old, would see the land of his birth. He had been so small when she'd taken him away. But it was the land that he would someday rule. There was no question that Caesarion would be *her* heir, though she was still uneasy about Octavius' position in Caesar's life.

Caesar made his plans and they were announced. He and his armies would leave Rome on the nineteenth of March. Cleopatra said that she would leave soon after. A ship was already on its way from Alexandria. She wanted to wait until Ptolemy was well enough to travel.

Early in March Cleopatra was examining some of the papyrus rolls, or books, she had brought with her. She wanted to decide which ones she would take back to Alexandria. There was a knock on her door and Apollodorus entered. He told the Queen that Ammonius wished to have a word with her.

The wealthy banker entered slowly. Cleopatra noticed that he was growing more feeble.

"Gracious Majesty," said the old man.

"Good Ammonius, be seated," said the Queen.

"I crave Your Majesty's pardon for intruding," he said, "but I thought I should tell you what happened this morning. Or have you already heard?"

Cleopatra shook her head.

Ammonius then told her that while on his way to
the senate Caesar had been stopped by the shrill cry
of a soothsayer.

"They often try to speak to him," said Cleopatra. "I
don't know why. He never listens to them, and he
teases me when I do."

"He heard what this one had to say," Ammonius
continued. "The soothsayer told him to beware the
Ides of March."

"The Ides of March!" the Queen exclaimed. "That
is the fifteenth day of March—next week."

Ammonius sighed heavily. "Do you not see what it
means, Highness? Everyone in Rome knows that Caesar
leaves on the nineteenth. The plotters may be planning to work fast."

"Do you know more that you are not saying?"
Cleopatra demanded.

"I know nothing else. Be assured that I will do my
best to find out. But you must caution Caesar doubly."

"I do it every day," said Cleopatra, "but I will try
again as soon as you can tell me something definite.
Vague threats do not touch him."

"These are more than vague threats," said Ammonius. "I am no soothsayer but I can see that there is
trouble ahead for Caesar."

On the twelfth of March Ammonius came to see
Cleopatra again. By now he had heard that there was
indeed a serious conspiracy to assassinate Caesar, who
had been made Dictator for life as a token of the
people's esteem. Because of that, only death could
ever remove him from his present power.

Ammonius was certain that Cassius was the leader
of the group against Caesar. This did not surprise

Cleopatra. She was sure that Brutus was in it, too.

On the next day, which was the thirteenth of March, Caesar sent Madrian to Cleopatra with a note and a gift. The present was a pair of amethyst earrings to match a ring he had already given her. The note said that he would dine with her the following night without fail. They had been invited to a dinner party at the house of Marcus Lepidus.

Lepidus was a general and an old friend of Caesar's. He was one of the few Cleopatra still liked and trusted.

Cleopatra wrote her reply at once so that Madrian could carry it back to Caesar.

"Now, Madrian," she said, giving him the sealed note, "I charge you again, do not leave him. Watch everything that he eats and drinks. Be always within call."

"Are you not worried by what the soothsayer said?" asked Madrian.

"I am worried by many things, Madrian."

"Do not fear, Adored Majesty," the little man boasted. "Nothing will hurt the Master while Madrian is alive."

"Then take care of yourself." Cleopatra smiled, grateful for his loyalty.

On the night of March 14th Cleopatra went with Caesar to Lepidus' house as they had arranged. The evening was a pleasant one. The guests were merry. Caesar was in an excellent humor. Mark Antony was there and made everyone laugh with his stories at the dinner table. For a while Cleopatra forgot her fears and enjoyed herself.

But after dinner an incident occurred that changed

her cheerful mood. One of the guests asked Lepidus what was the best way to die.

Before Lepidus could answer Caesar's voice rang out. "The best death is always sudden."

Antony was watching the Queen as he always did. He saw a strange look come into her face. She had been laughing only a moment before.

He went to her at once. "What is the matter?" he asked.

"I will be glad when tomorrow has come and gone."

"Tomorrow?" Antony looked puzzzled. "What is to-morrow?"

"The Ides of March," Cleopatra answered.

"And is that an important day for you?"

"I hope not," said the Queen of Egypt.

She knew that Antony had not been with Caesar on the morning of the soothsayer's prophecy. And he, like Caesar, had little use for fortunetellers.

Shortly after, Caesar and Cleopatra left the gathering. They went back to her villa and sat in the upstairs room, the one they both liked best. Caesar looked about the handsome room with its soft lamps and objects of beauty.

"Soon we shall be in a tent again," he said. "Will you mind?"

"I wish we were there now," Cleopatra said firmly.

"Are you still troubled about the soothsayer?" Caesar shook his head. "How can you, who are so wise, be so silly about that?"

"My country is older than yours," said Cleopatra. "We know there are people who can see beyond the veil of time."

"I thought you were a Macedonian," said Caesar,

teasing. "Now you are talking like an Egyptian."

"It is a curious thing," she admitted. "Since I have been living in Rome I have begun to think of myself as an Egyptian. All those years that the Ptolemies have been in Egypt. . . . I see them, I feel them. I had to leave Egypt to become an Egyptian."

"And when you are back there you will find yourself a Roman, I suppose," Caesar said, laughing at her.

Cleopatra rose and paced the room. "How can I make you listen to me?" she asked.

"I will hear no more about soothsayers."

"There is more than that." She spoke urgently. "I tell you they plan to kill you before you leave Rome. Why not stay here in the villa until it is time to leave for Parthia?"

"There is too much to do," said Caesar. "Besides, they can plot all they want. Romans like to plot. But they won't kill me. They don't dare. People try to warn me but I will not listen. I wish you would not."

"At least do not go to the senate tomorrow," Cleopatra pleaded desperately. "Just stay away tomorrow. One day doesn't matter."

Caesar could see that she was deeply upset. Her face was pale and her eyes were filled with tears.

"Perhaps I will not go tomorrow," he said. "I will decide in the morning. Sleep well and don't worry. I shall send Madrian with a note for you to have with your breakfast."

He left the villa and drove back across the river into Rome. Cleopatra stood in the doorway and listened to the horses' hoofbeats and the sounds of the chariot wheels until she heard them no more. Then

she undressed and went to bed. But she could not sleep. Toward dawn there began a terrible storm. Thunder seemed to shake the house and lightning constantly lit up the sky. A heavy, pounding rain began to fall.

Cleopatra arose and went into Caesarion's room. She thought that the storm might have awakened him. He was in his bed, sound asleep, one hand holding fast to a toy.

Seeing that a lamp was lit at Ptolemy's house near by, she decided to go over and see if he was all right. The heavy rain had stopped.

She drew a cloak over her nightdress and went out into the garden. It was not yet light outside but she could see well enough in the dark. She took a step and stopped. Madrian's tiny body lay outstretched on the damp ground, a dagger thrust into his heart. As she knelt, a quick glance told her the worst. Little Madrian was dead.

CHAPTER XVIII

The Ides of March

Cleopatra's fears were justified. Julius Caesar was stabbed to death on the morning of March 15th.

Apollodorus was in Rome when the terrible event occurred. The Queen had sent him to Caesar with a note reporting what had happened to Madrian. She had also begged Caesar to come to her at once and not to go to the senate.

But Caesar was never to see that last message from Cleopatra. By the time Apollodorus reached the Dictator's house, he had departed. Cassius had sent a man whom Caesar trusted with the message that it was urgent for him to come to the senate as soon as possible.

In the meantime the conspirators made sure that Mark Antony would be kept away from the senate. They invented problems of state to occupy him near by. Cassius had worked out the plan with care. He took no chance that something might go wrong. There might not be another opportunity.

Apollodorus hurried along the busy streets, hoping to overtake Caesar. There were crowds of people outside the senate. They surrounded Caesar as he made his way forward. People were pushing to get to him, to see him, to greet him. Some were shoving petitions at him. That was a Roman custom. These were written on parchment and requested Caesar's help in one cause or another.

But one of the scrolls placed into his hand was not a petition. It was a warning, written by a friend named Artemidorus. On it were the details of the trap into which Caesar was walking, together with the names of the conspirators.

However, Caesar was given no chance to read it. Cassius and Brutus had joined him and were already guiding him past the mass of people toward the long hall of the senate.

Just outside the senate entry, Caesar suddenly spied the soothsayer.

"Well, Soothsayer, the Ides of March are come," said Caesar lightly.

"They are come, but they are not past!" was the reply.

Cassar laughed and went on inside. He was in good spirits and responded to the greetings of those who gathered about him.

He walked to the end of the marble hall and there he paused, hemmed in by a group of senators and others who had joined the group. He had walked into the trap but was not yet aware of it.

He stood at the base of a large statue of Pompey, once his friend and later his deadly rival. As a typical example of Caesar's capacity to love and to forgive, he had ordered the statue to be erected there in honor of that great Roman. But while he stood there, discussing important matters with Brutus and Cassius,

one of the men at the rear of the group stepped in closer and pulled down Caesar's toga to expose his neck. It was the signal.

The first blow was struck by Casca, a friend and aide of Cassius. He attempted to plunge a dagger into Caesar's neck, but he was clumsy and nervous and the blow was not deep. Caesar turned around astonished and shouted, "Traitor!"

At this, the pack closed in. There were many conspirators and every man had pledged he would deliver
a blow. In that way all would be equally guilty. Even
in this horrible act, Roman justice performed accord-
ing to its code.

Caesar was, of course, unarmed. But he fought and
resisted furiously, using the thick folds of his toga
against the rapid dagger and sword blows that fell on

him. As the seconds passed, no help arrived. Everyone watching from a distance was paralyzed by the
sight.

Then Caesar, as he made a tortured turn, saw Brutus striking at him with a short sword. Unbelievingly
he cried, "You too, Brutus!" and resisted no longer.

Instead, he drew himself up as well as he could and
covered his face with his toga so that no one could
see his agony and his grief at this betrayal. Then he
fell.

There at the foot of Pompey's statue Julius Caesar
died with the courage and dignity that he had shown
every day of his life.

The conspirators fled, and even those in the senate
who had witnessed the deed but had no share in it ran
terrified from the building. They wanted to be no part
of this hideous event. For a long time Caesar's body
lay there untouched, his face still covered.

The news spread like flame on dry wood. People
were stunned and horrified. Apollodorus heard amazed
shouts and screams: "Great Caesar is dead!"

The confusion and turmoil was still great when
Mark Antony, having heard the news, arrived at the
scene. People fell silent at the sight of Caesar's greatest friend.

Cassius had wanted to do away with Antony along
with Caesar. Knowing that Antony would never turn
against Caesar, Cassius felt that he was a dangerous
threat to the assassination plot.

But Brutus, strangely enough, had insisted that Antony's life be spared. He had argued that Antony was
not a tyrant but a loyal Roman, a good consul and a
superb soldier, well liked by the people. It would be

possible to explain to the masses that Caesar's death was desirable for the good of Rome. But it would not be possible to justify Antony's.

Now, even in his grief and shock, Mark Antony took charge. He ordered a litter made and summoned three slaves to carry it. Slowly and tenderly they raised Caesar's body from the stone floor and placed it on the litter. The slaves carried the body to Caesar's house through the hushed streets. Stunned, weeping people watched from their houses. In that manner, Caesar left the senate, where he had served the people of Rome so well. He was fifty-six years old, the greatest man on earth, and he was dead.

The Queen of Egypt heard the shocking news even before Apollodorus managed to get back. It had spread swiftly up and down each bank of the Tiber.

Mark Antony was unable to come to Cleopatra until late in the evening. He had had much to do. He had investigated all the details of the murder. He had made arrangements for a state funeral. He had looked through Caesar's private papers and read his will. When all was done he came to tell Cleopatra what had been accomplished.

The Queen's house was dim and silent. Only a few lamps were lit. The air was hushed and sad. The Queen held out her hand to Mark Antony. It was a small hand and it was very cold. He clasped it within his own.

She was as pale as ivory. Her eyes were so sad and empty that Antony could scarcely bear looking into them. But there were no other signs that her world was shattered. She was, as ever, straight and proud.

Antony told her what he had found out and what

arrangements he had made. He explained that the plotters had arranged for him to be detained away from the senate so that he was not with his commander when he died. Otherwise he would have fought with him to the death.

"Brutus has made a mistake to let me live," Antony vowed. "I promise you I shall avenge this murder!"

"You were his good friend, Mark Antony."

"I am also yours," he answered. "And I am fearful for Your Majesty's safety."

"I am not afraid," she replied. In her grief, she had given no thought to herself.

Charmian hurried into the room. She was trembling. "Forgive me, Divinity, but there are many men—soldiers—in the garden!"

Antony explained quickly. "They are my men. This house is to be guarded day and night until you leave Rome, Majesty."

Cleopatra looked at him surprised. He was behaving like Caesar. She was reminded of the night when Caesar had told her that her quarters were to be protected from harm at the hands of Ptolemy. Now it seemed she had new enemies and a new protector.

"Believe me, it is necessary," Antony added.

He didn't want to alarm her, but the feeling against her in Rome was bitter. Many were saying that she was responsible for Caesar's death because of her ambitions for him. The conspirators hated and feared her. Brutus had never approved of her. Cassius felt that she had snubbed him, and he would be only too pleased to see her dead. There was no telling now what might happen.

"By tomorrow your ship at Ostia will be ready,"

said Antony. "It would be well for you to leave on it at once."

"I will not go until my brother, the King, is able to travel with me," said Cleopatra quietly. "He has not been well."

"I beg Your Majesty to make haste."

"I have no wish to linger here, I assure you," the Queen replied. "But I must also find out what arrangements Caesar has made for our son."

Antony's face was troubled. No provision had been made for Caesarion. Caesar had not even mentioned him in the will. He had never been able to get around to it. His lands and gardens he left to the Roman people to be used as public parks. Every Roman citizen inherited seventy-five drachmas (about $100). The rest of his fortune went to his family.

The worst news of all was that Octavius was named as Caesar's only and official son and heir.

Cleopatra was hurt and shocked. Antony tried to comfort her by saying that it was not a recent will. Surely if he had not been killed, Caesar would have changed it in Caesarion's favor.

"We shall never know," Cleopatra said.

"I know what Caesar would now have wanted me to do," Antony replied. "Caesarion is his rightful heir. But he is only three years old. He cannot rule for several years."

Cleopatra was silent, so he went on.

"I ask you to name me his legal Roman guardian and let me act as regent for him until he is of age."

The Queen considered this. She wanted to leave Rome. Someone must continue to look after Caesarion's

interests. No one else would be so true a friend as
Mark Antony. She was grateful for such a suggestion
in this difficult hour.

"I appoint you as the Roman regent of my son,"
she said, removing from one of her delicate fingers a
ring bearing the royal scarab. He accepted it from her
as a token of this pledge.

"First we have a long account to settle with the
assassins," Antony declared. "Then Caesar's child will
come into his own."

She did not speak. Looking at him, she saw again
the resolute rescuer of her father. Now he was looking after her son. She had faith that things would
happen as he said.

They talked then of other plans that needed to be
made. Finally Mark Antony left. The long day was
done. The Ides of March were over.

CHAPTER XIX

Farewell to a Roman

Terror and lawlessness swept the city after Caesar's death. No one felt safe. Few people went out at night. Citizens—especially those of importance—carried swords with them at all times. The taverns were empty. The shops were closed. All Rome waited anxiously to see what would happen next.

The conspirators also remained in their houses. Some had fled from the city. Whenever a few of them met to make plans they quarreled among themselves. All decisions were put off until after Caesar's state funeral. That would be a tense day.

Cleopatra had no callers except for Antony and old Ammonius. No one else was brave enough to be seen entering the villa. The Queen herself never left it. Even when Caesar was alive she had rarely gone into Rome. Now there was no reason to go.

The night before Caesar's funeral, Mark Antony came to see the Queen. It was very late. He apologized for the hour of his visit. But he had something important to tell her. Earlier in the day he had gone to visit Brutus. Antony had heard that Brutus was going to make an oration at the funeral. He told Brutus that he also intended to speak. To Antony's surprise, Brutus agreed to this.

Later Antony learned from informers that Cassius had protested. He insisted that it was Antony's intention to avenge the death of Caesar. Cassius wanted Brutus to keep him from talking to the people of Rome at the funeral. He declared it could lead only to trouble for them all.

But Brutus had disagreed. "Have no fear," he said to Cassius. "I will speak first and the people of Rome know me as a man of honor. I shall let them know our excellent reasons for what we did. We have saved Rome from a tyrant. They will understand that and be grateful."

Antony then told the Queen that her plan to attend the funeral in the forum on the following day should be canceled. "There might be disorder and trouble, which could endanger you, even if you are not recognized," Antony warned. "And if you are seen, no one can guess what the outcome might be. A mob is a wild animal."

Cleopatra thanked him for his anxiety on her behalf.

At high noon on the following day, the forum was filled with thousands and thousands of people. They were strangely quiet as they waited for the ceremonies to begin. The day was clear. A fresh breeze was blowing. The sky was the soft blue of early spring.

Caesar's body was lying on a great white marble slab in the center of the square. It was covered with a velvet cloth of royal purple, on which rested a simple wreath of bay leaves, the symbol of victory.

First the priests and temple officials spoke the pray-

ers and incantations that invoked the presence of the
gods. Then, suddenly and unexpectedly, Brutus, in a
toga of mourning, mounted a stand near the body.
There was a swelling murmur from the massed crowd.
But it subsided at once as he raised his arms and his
rich, trained voice filled the whole area with his words.
The silence was absolute, for Brutus was greatly respected. The tradition of his honor and his services to
the state placed him above politics. No one wanted to
miss a word he had to say.

As he went on, the great crowd responded to him.
He seemed to be making them believe that Caesar had
become too ambitious for the good of the Roman
state. It was incredible that this cold, cruel man could
be making the people accept the murder of the brilliant leader who had loved them.

When he had finished, he looked about him, confident. His victory with the mob seemed complete. Many
even cheered him as he moved away from the mortal
remains of the man he had claimed to love and whom
he had killed. With the fickleness of all mobs, the
people of Rome were ready to turn their backs on the
memory of a man who had done so much for them.

Now it was Antony's turn to speak. The mass of
people, many thousands of them, fell silent again.
They filled to overflowing the great square of the
forum, the many streets that led off it, as well as every
rooftop.

Antony was not a trained orator, as Brutus was.
But his soldier's voice was powerful, trained in the
giving of commands. Before he spoke, he waited respectfully as Brutus left the scene. Then he looked
long at the motionless body of the dead man. At last

he looked down upon the countless upturned faces, and began to talk.

Shakespeare's version of Antony's speech makes it one of the most remarkable ever delivered. Though written for the theatre, the substance of it is no doubt very much like the original, for the great playwright studied the records of the event reported by ancient historians.

"Friends, Romans, countrymen, lend me your ears," Antony began. What he then said was very like the man who said it—simple, forceful, direct, full of feeling. Step by step, he led his vast audience away from thoughts of Caesar's ambition to recollections of what Caesar had accomplished.

Gradually and skillfully, Antony moved his listeners to tears, to cheers and finally to shouts of rage at the killers. Then, sensing his victory, Antony made doubly sure of it. He read to the assembled thousands the terms of Caesar's will, which had been so loving and generous to every one of them.

Upon hearing this the crowd, which had been orderly until now, became wild. Caesar was no longer a tyrant who deserved to die; he was again their hero. "Death to the assassins!" they shouted. They would not allow Caesar's body to be moved away to the customary burial ground outside the city. Instead they insisted that their dead leader should be given a funeral pyre right in the heart of the city he had loved. Three of his old veterans set fire to the purple cloth and at once the populace threw onto it all their outer garments, then all the wood they could lay hands on. Musicians ran forward and added their instruments to

the mounting flames. Even the children became so excited that they tossed in their toys.

Every Roman appeared to be seized with a desire to show his love and gratitude to Caesar. The scene became a sea of howling people. The flames leaped higher and higher. The clear air was darkened with smoke. The sun was hidden and day seemed to turn into night.

The mob spirit now spread through the city. Rome became a mass of excitement; everyone was seized with a desire for vengeance. Brutus and Cassius were hunted down but, warned in time, they had fled.

CHAPTER XX

Farewell to Rome

Great personal problems now faced Cleopatra. The Roman government which would have to decide Caesarion's position was in a state of disorder and uncertainty. Nothing could be settled. Brutus, as well as Cassius and all the known conspirators, stayed hidden deep in the Italian countryside. The senate seemed powerless, torn by rival factions.

Gradually Mark Antony, with the aid of the Roman general Lepidus, who was also a senator, came into full charge. As Caesar's friends and men of proved ability, they were trusted by the populace. This support won for them the backing of the senate in restoring order. In effect, they quickly became the leaders of the Roman state.

People everywhere began to wonder what would happen when Octavius returned to Rome. Antony and the Queen of Egypt were wondering the same thing. Octavius had been on military duty in Greece for some time, but it was known that he had left at once for Rome upon hearing of Caesar's death.

Doubtless Octavius had learned that he had been named sole heir in Caesar's will. Just what that spelled in respect to his inheriting any of Caesar's titles and powers was a question. After all, Caesar had not died a king. But there was no doubt that Octavius would make an effort to claim as much of Caesar's power as possible. Above all it seemed certain he would oppose Antony's reporting to the senate that Caesar had acknowledged Caesarion as his child. With that in mind it was necessary to act without further delay.

On the morning of March 25th, ten days after Caesar's death, Mark Antony went to the senate early. He had decided to tell them that day about Caesarion. He knew it would be difficult. They had read Caesar's will; they all knew Octavius. And under Roman law it would be impossible to recognize Caesar's Egyptian marriage. In fact, many doubted that one had ever taken place.

But Antony had no chance to carry out his plan, for when he entered his private chamber to prepare himself for addressing the senate, there stood Octavius, waiting for him.

Antony would rather have seen anyone else in the world at that moment. However, he greeted Octavius pleasantly; and Caesar's heir, pleased by this reception, responded in the same manner. Antony was a man of great influence, and his friendship was important at this critical time.

Octavius was full of confidence. As Caesar's only official heir, the senate was bound to support him in his claim for increased position and authority. He was only nineteen years old, but he was ambitious. It was clear to Antony that Octavius had big plans for the future, and that he would let nothing stand in their way.

The young man declared that he intended to make known at once to the senate his arrival in Rome. To this Antony could only comply. Octavius' enmity was something to avoid. Nothing could be gained by raising the question of Caesarion at such a moment as this. The presence in the senate of Caesar's legal heir would only complicate things.

After he had been in Rome a week, Octavius rode out to visit the Queen of Egypt. He had been surprised to learn that she was still in Rome. He knew that her gardens had been left to the people along with Caesar's other lands. He had heard too that many citizens were resentful that Cleopatra had not yet left the city.

But Cleopatra had been unable to go home. Her brother Ptolemy had been growing steadily worse. Nothing that the doctors did seemed to help or reduce his fever.

On the afternoon that Octavius came to see her, Cleopatra had arranged that Ptolemy be moved to her house so that she could be nearer to him. Octavius found her greatly upset about her brother's condition. She seemed to have changed. He thought that she looked tired and worried. She was dressed more simply. Her manner was quiet. Her beautiful voice was so low that he could barely hear her. She was a tragic figure in the half-empty house. But Octavius felt no pity for her.

Cleopatra also detected a change in Octavius. She scarcely recognized him. The thin, pallid boy had vanished. There was now authority and confidence in the young man who sat talking to her. His eyes were colder and unfriendlier than ever.

He asked to see Caesarion. Iras brought the boy in. Apollodorus was in the background in case he might be needed. None of them trusted Octavius.

Cleopatra watched Octavius studying Caesar's real son. What were his thoughts? She couldn't tell. His was a closed and secret face.

"I regret that Your Majesty's brother is ill," Octavius said politely. "I hope that he will soon recover."

"Thank you. We are all most eager to return home."

"You are wise," said Octavius. "Rome is not a safe place these days."

Cleopatra sensed a threat behind the words.

"Without your uncle," she replied, "the whole world is not a safe place."

"I will come to see you before you leave," Octavius said.

"You must not trouble," said the Queen. "It is a long drive and this is a quiet house now."

"As Your Majesty pleases." Octavius bowed and left Cleopatra's house.

Cleopatra called for Apollodorus.

"Do not leave Caesarion for a second," she said to him. "He is in danger now that Octavius has returned. Great danger."

"I will not let him out of my sight, Divinity," promised Apollodorus. "No harm will come to him."

Then Cleopatra went to her brother's room. Ptolemy was making an effort to sit up, but when he saw his sister he fell back on his pillow with a little smile. He was terribly pale.

"Sister," Ptolemy said, "do you know what I want so much to see?"

Cleopatra shook her head. She took his hand and sat beside him.

"The glass makers who have their shops on the street behind our palace."

"It will be good to see them again," she agreed.

"Oh, Sister, will they still be there?"

"Of course they will. Everything will be the same. Everyone will be waiting to see you."

"Then I will go to sleep now," Ptolemy said. "I am so tired."

"Sleep, little brother," said the Queen softly.

Tears came to her eyes. She saw the doctors coming into the room. But she did not need them to tell her what she already knew. Poor little Ptolemy would never see his beloved Alexandria again. He was dying.

Two weeks later Ptolemy was dead. The Queen of Egypt was no longer bound in any way to Italy. In the early morning of April 15th, a month after Caesar's death, she went to the seaport of Ostia and boarded the Egyptian vessel that would take her home.

Mark Antony went to the ship with her. He wanted to be sure that she and Caesarion left safely. He promised the Queen that he would keep her informed of all the happenings in Rome. He would not forget, he said, that he was Caesarion's regent.

"We trust you, Mark Antony," said Cleopatra.

He bowed over her hand. On her finger she had the huge amethyst that Caesar had given her. In her ears were the amethyst earrings that had been his last present. And on her head was the little coronet that she had worn to the triumphs. It was the only crown Caesar ever gave her, after all.

The morning was gray and chill. There was a fine mist in the air. The Queen drew her cloak closer to her. Then she turned to say good-by.

"Farewell, Mark Antony," she said.

He raised his arm in the Roman salute. "Farewell, Great Queen."

Then the ship cast off, but Cleopatra's feelings were far different from what they had been on her departure from Alexandria two years before. No exciting cries, no thrill. Even the day was gloomy.

Cleopatra told Iras to put Caesarion to bed in his cabin. She stayed on deck alone and watched the Italian shore until it disappeared. How happily she had arrived there! How eager to see Caesar! Now she was leaving. And she would never see Caesar again.

"Good-by, Caesar's land," she whispered into the wind. "You never will be my land, but you will be my son's. He will return in triumph to claim the throne that will be his."

Back on the shore Mark Antony looked out for a long time at the great ship growing smaller as it headed for Alexandria. At last he turned to go. He could no longer see the bit of bright purple that was her cloak. But he could still hear in his ears the sound of that soft, sweet voice. "Farewell, Mark Antony."

He looked back once more. "We will meet again, Egypt," the tall, bronzed man called across the sea that was dividing them.

Part Three

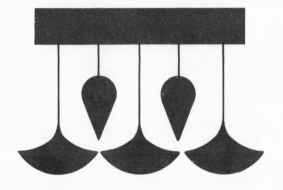

CHAPTER XXI

The Golden Galley

Two long and busy years passed before Cleopatra saw Mark Antony again. During that time she was occupied with ruling her country. This she did well. Trade flourished. Egyptian goods were in demand. Her beloved Nile flowed green and majestic through a prosperous and peaceful land.

The Queen and her little son were now the only remaining members of the Ptolemy line. She decided to make Caesarion a king, so that they might rule jointly. This would remind the world of his royal position. Also it could protect them both against possible political enemies at home or abroad.

The boy was very like his father. He was quick and bright. No one saw him without being charmed by him. Sometimes, as Cleopatra showed him the beauties of Alexandria and heard the people cheering him, she thought of Octavius. Her smile would vanish. She was well aware that the existence of Caesar's actual son must be hateful to the adopted one.

Would the hatred and jealousy of Octavius stretch across the sea? Would he make an effort to have Caesarion murdered? Cleopatra found comfort in the fact that the now powerful Mark Antony was pledged to protect him.

The handsome Roman wrote to her occasionally. They were not the brilliant letters that Caesar had written. Nor did the Queen treasure them as she did Caesar's. But she was pleased to hear from Antony and always replied. He was her friend in Rome and, if she handled things well, Egypt would have no trouble from that direction.

But it was Julius Caesar who was still constantly in her thoughts. There was so much in the palace that reminded her of him. Because of him she had her throne. Because of him her country was the only one in this part of the world free from Roman domination and taxation.

All the gifts he had given her were kept in special locked cases. She would often open these and look at the lovely things and remember the occasions they marked. But since her return to her own land, she wore only the elaborate, heavy jewels that had belonged to the Ptolemaic queens for generations past.

When she thought of Rome, she shivered. She would miss Julius Caesar for the rest of her life. But she would never miss Rome. For her it had been a city of tragedy.

Meanwhile the two years were full ones for Mark Antony. True to his vow, he had set about avenging Caesar's murder. Brutus and Cassius had fled from Rome and were busy getting allies and support for themselves in far-off lands where discontent against Rome made it possible. Antony was organizing the legions to pursue and defeat them wherever they were found.

151 The Golden Galley

In the meantime the government of Rome had been reorganized and made more firm. Antony joined with young Octavius and General Lepidus in what was called the Triumvirate. The three of them now ruled the republic. It was not a situation much to the liking of either Antony or Octavius, who would have preferred to do it alone. But being a triumvir was a step toward total control, so each accepted his new position and waited.

When Antony had formed and equipped eight legions he was ready to move, in company with Octavius, in pursuit of Brutus and Cassius. By now these two, along with others who had been connected with the conspiracy against Caesar, had gathered a considerable army in Greece. It was made up of nations and groups throughout the Mediterranean who were eager to escape from Roman bondage.

Cleopatra watched these events with growing anxiety. Victory by her enemies in the coming conflict could seriously affect Egypt. Her problem was increased when Cassius sent word demanding her support. She paid no attention to this. However, the officer in command of her fleet was so impressed by the rise of Cassius' power that he ordered the Egyptian fleet to sail to his aid. Wanting to be on the winning side, he did this without even consulting the Queen.

Apollodorus awakened Cleopatra in the middle of the night to bring her this news. She was able to recall the fleet and promptly imprison the offending admiral. But anxious weeks followed as the whole Mediterranean world watched and waited for the outcome of the contest that lay ahead.

The decisive battle came in Greece, on its eastern

This plan would allow Cleopatra time to make the necessary preparations for the journey, and it would give Mark Antony a perfect opportunity to see her again. This was desirable for a number of reasons. Egypt had a small but well-equipped army and navy. For political and military purposes, he wished to make sure of their support. The personal reasons were even more pressing. Antony wanted to see for himself whether the Queen of the Nile was still as beautiful and fascinating as he remembered her.

Cleopatra received Antony's invitation with satisfaction. Her constant concern with the welfare of her son and her country was at the heart of this. Also, Antony had always been a romantic image in her life. Now, with the crown of victory on him, he seemed more romantic than ever.

While Antony busied himself with preparations for a difficult campaign, Cleopatra made ready for the voyage to Tarsus. She knew that Antony would be impressed by Egyptian splendor. It was her intention to arrive for the meeting with him in the most elegant manner.

One of her state galleys was newly and richly decorated. Its stern was gilded, its oars were silvered and new sails of royal purple were mounted. When it came time to set forth for Tarsus, thirty ships of her fleet formed the company. A large retinue came along, including musicians, entertainers and her best cooks. She did not forget Antony's liking for Egyptian food.

Cleopatra wondered what to expect. Antony's letter requesting her presence had been a formal one. There had been no recent indication from him that he remembered his warm declarations of friendship. It was essential now for her to make a memorable impression on him.

When she had first met Caesar she had been unadorned and simply dressed. But she would now appear before Antony in the role of a dazzling oriental monarch. Her costumes, her jewels, the people of her court would present a spectacle such as Mark Antony had never seen.

As the Roman came aboard her galley, the air was perfumed. The entire fleet glittered with the fabulous effect of thousands of colored lights. The Queen was attired in draperies of blue silk; at her throat and wrists and ears glistened priceless ornaments.

All of this merely served to emphasize Cleopatra's beauty and allure. Mark Antony was enthralled by her again, just as he had been in Rome. And now there would be no Caesar to stand between them.

They dined at a feast that the historians of the time have well recorded. It is recorded too that Mark Antony did not conceal his immediate infatuation. If Cleopatra had set a trap she had set it well. Or perhaps it was Antony who was all too ready to walk into it.

The party lasted until dawn. The Queen had provided entertainment for her guests which proved to be fully as successful as the marvelous food. Finally the guests departed and, when all the others had gone, Mark Antony remained.

The Roman and the Egyptian Queen stood at the prow of the golden galley. The sun was rising in the morning sky. A new day was dawning, and a new life had begun for Cleopatra of Egypt.

CHAPTER XXII

The Falling Star

The romantic meeting between Antony and Cleopatra had an immediate effect on his military plans. To the shocked surprise of everybody, the Roman did not return to his preparations for war against the rebellion in Syria. Instead, he returned to Alexandria with the Queen and settled down there for many months of gay and luxurious living.

Rome sent ambassadors to urge his early return. He was needed there. Octavius was quarreling with many prominent Romans, including his own brother. This was the situation that Antony had hoped for. If he had gone home then, he would have been given a triumph, and his successful return might well have meant the end of Octavius. But he did not return.

Instead, the ambassadors brought back tales of an Antony who had taken to wearing Grecian costumes in public. This was an unthinkable thing for a great Roman general to do. The same ambassadors also carried with them rumors that Antony had married Cleopatra. They reported that he was presenting the Queen with gifts of lands and territories that were the property of Rome.

There was no doubt in the mind of anyone that these two were in love. Antony was in a state of enchantment by this woman "of infinite variety," as Shakespeare has described her. Cleopatra was stirred by his strength and vitality. She found comfort in having again a powerful ally who meant such complete protection.

The difference between Caesar and Antony was a marked one. Caesar had wisdom; Antony had force. Caesar had wit; Mark Antony had humor. Caesar had intellectual curiosity; Antony wanted merely to be amused and entertained. But both were brave and courageous.

By turning his back on the Syrian uprising, Antony had made a serious mistake. This was the moment in his career, after the brilliant victory at Philippi, when he should have swept on to new heights of conquest. But he let the moment go.

Not only did he continue to ignore the rebellion in Syria; he left other matters throughout Asia in mounting confusion. It became a critical situation for the empire. He paid no attention to the urgent appeals he was receiving from Rome. He delighted in the ravishing Cleopatra and the charms and luxury of Alexandria.

Years before, Caesar had found fault with Antony's irresponsible behavior, his debts and his drinking. For a while Antony had changed. He was capable of hard work and was a splendid officer. But in the silkened, perfumed atmosphere of the Egyptian palace, the man of battle whom Caesar had admired turned again into the pleasure lover whom Caesar had despised.

Cleopatra, clever as she was, seemed not to foresee

the disaster that lay ahead. Apparently she did not want Antony to leave her for an instant. If they had parted at Tarsus, she would have lived a life of peace and dignity, and he might have gone on to a glory that matched Caesar's.

But she loved Antony, and no doubt she felt that his nearness protected her and her son. However, the very opposite was true. Cleopatra, who had never been liked in Rome because of her hold on Caesar, now was bitterly blamed for the conduct of Mark Antony.

By spring, the situation in Rome had reached a point where he no longer could delay his return home. He heard that Octavius had rid himself of Lepidus and stood almost alone in his authority. It was a threat Antony could not fail to recognize. Even in his infatuated state he realized that if he did not go back and reestablish himself he might lose all.

Faced with reality, Antony decided he wanted power even more than he wanted Cleopatra. So, at last, he arrived back in Rome. He found that it was none too soon. Octavius' power and popularity were increasing. He had lost his early shyness. He showed new qualities of strength and character. More dangerous to Antony, he had become an expert politician.

Caesar's adopted son did not hesitate to show his hostility to the returned Antony. He was well aware that Antony might some day support Caesarion against him. Octavius had succeeded in deposing Lepidus as an effective member of the Triumvirate. Perhaps he could do the same to Antony.

But, despite Antony's behavior, Rome was glad of his return and quickly forgave him. For a time after his arrival it looked as if the government might split into two rival camps. But gradually peaceful relations were restored between Octavius and Antony. Octavius had a sister, a gentle and beautiful girl named Octavia, of whom he was very fond. Octavia, in turn, greatly admired Mark Antony. When a marriage between them was suggested it seemed the perfect solution to a difficult situation. All Rome was delighted when the marriage finally took place.

The news of this marriage came as a blow to Cleopatra. First she was furious, then despairing. But gradually her Ptolemy training and blood gave her comfort. She realized that one had to do things for reasons of state that had nothing to do with the heart. She would bide her time. She would have faith in the love of Antony.

It was to be a long wait that Cleopatra endured. For more than three years Antony and Octavius lived and worked together in harmony. The influence of the lovely Octavia had much to do with this. She loved her husband and she loved her brother. It was a strong tie between these two natural enemies.

From her old friend Ammonius, Cleopatra received reports throughout this time. Octavius was becoming increasingly popular with the people. He went on many short campaigns that ensured the security of Rome. Meanwhile Antony was neglecting his duties and drinking too much in the public taverns. But then he redeemed himself again by a short war in Syria from which he came back to a triumph.

Now the fight for supremacy became a tug of war between the two powerful leaders. Not even Octavia could bring peace into this quarrelsome situation.

Finally, early in the winter of 37 B.C., Antony left Rome. He went to Antioch on the Mediterranean coast of Syria. It was south of Tarsus, the scene of his memorable meeting with Cleopatra. His announced purpose in going there was to lead an army into Parthia, deep in Asia Minor. This was the home of the many tribes, largely known as Persians, who were resisting Roman domination. They had even been sweeping into the coastal provinces of Asia Minor and threatening Roman forces there.

This was an important mission. At least it would have been if Antony had carried it through. But the spell of Cleopatra was upon him. Once again he sent a message asking her to join him in Antioch.

To Cleopatra this seemed the most triumphant moment of her life. She forgave him for the long years she had been forced to endure without him. In Antioch they resumed together the romantic and exotic life they had shared in Alexandria. Despite the existence of Octavia and the Roman laws against having more than one wife, Antony married Cleopatra in a public ceremony, followed by a great celebration. She was dressed as the goddess Venus, and he was attired as Dionysus, Greek god of wine and fertility.

In the days that followed he presented her with the Island of Crete and other eastern provinces belonging to Rome. She became in this way the ruler, with her son, of more territory than she could have won in a successful war. The effect of all this on Rome was one of outrage.

At last, after many delays, Antony declared himself ready to carry war into Parthia for the suppression of an uprising in that remote land. In this belief he was mistaken. His venture was badly organized owing to his neglect of it. But he desired to demonstrate to Cleopatra and the world that he was the equal of Caesar.

He proceeded on the long march through Armenia into the deepest regions of Asia Minor. His troops were poorly equipped and ill-trained for the terrain they had to cross. They carried heavy engines of war, such as battering rams. These impeded progress and were worthless against the swift Parthian cavalry that attacked Antony's infantry with arrows day after day.

Thousands of his men were killed or left wounded by the road. Many men deserted. Antony's promised allies dropped away from him, not wishing to be involved in a losing fight. Among these was the King of Armenia, who had promised strong support.

Without even reaching his final objective, Antony had to turn back. He had been terribly beaten and his army almost ceased to exist.

Cleopatra, who had gone home to Egypt, returned to Antioch to offer Antony comfort and help when he arrived there. He had now totally lost the favor of the people of Rome. They liked winners. Antony's fearful defeat in Parthia was a blow to Roman pride. His association with the Egyptian queen was doubly held against him.

Octavia, in spite of having been so humiliated by Antony, was still in love with him. She now made a final effort to save him. She sailed from Rome to Athens bringing with her money, arms and soldiers. She wrote to him that she was coming. She begged him to return to her so that she could settle matters between him and Octavius before it was too late.

Antony was with Cleopatra when the letter came.

He read it and was touched by Octavia's goodness.
Cleopatra herself was moved by the nobility of Octavia's action. But she made it clear to Antony that he
must choose between them. He wrote to Octavia and
told her he could not come to Athens at that time.
Moreover, he said that it would be unwise for her to
come to him at Antioch.

The meaning of his words was clear. Octavia was
broken-hearted when she read them. Even so, she sent
on to him the money, men and weapons she had
brought. Then she went back to Rome, where she did
her best to protect Antony from the rising hatred of
her brother, Octavius. But that would have been difficult—even for Octavia. Caesar's adopted son had come
to a pinnacle of power in Rome. The Triumvirate was
not renewed. Lepidus was somewhere in Africa, where
he would remain; and Antony would now be disposed
of by Octavius when the opportunity presented.

With the men and means provided by Octavia, Antony waged a quick war with the King of Armenia.
This was to punish him for his treachery during the
Parthian campaign. It was highly successful, and the
Armenian monarch was brought back in chains to be
shown in a triumph for Antony in Alexandria. It was
the first Roman triumph ever to be held away from
Rome.

Cleopatra herself, on this occasion, was given by
Antony the title of Queen of Kings. It was made
known that she had borne twins to Antony, a boy and
a girl named Cleopatra and Alexander. They were
given royal titles and made monarchs of new territories that Antony had acquired by his recent victory.
Caesarion's rule was also extended by Antony beyond

Egypt to include huge areas that Rome regarded as her natural right.

The issue with Octavius was now fully in the open. In 33 B.C. Antony, overconfident as always, decided to have an outright war with his rival. He and Cleopatra would bring the entire East against Octavius. If victorious, they could then form a mighty alliance with themselves at the head.

In Rome itself, sides were taken in the senate. Antony still had many friends there—or perhaps it was Octavius who had many enemies. Whichever it was, several senators came to see Antony at Ephesus, where he was now forming his army. They wanted to advise him, to help him.

But when they arrived, they were amazed to find that Cleopatra was also in Ephesus with Antony. They were more distressed to find out that no decisions were being made without her knowledge and her consent. Antony's friends beseeched him to make the Queen go back to Egypt. If a report reached Rome that Antony was now ruled by the woman who had become a symbol of evil to all Romans, he might never be able to return there.

Antony laughed at this. He did not wish to live without Cleopatra. He would not send her away. As for Rome, he was in no hurry to see it. When he decided to go back, he would know how to deal with the fickle heart of Rome.

During this time Octavius was preparing himself and his armies for action. He told the senate that a critical contest lay ahead. News of much support for Antony among the usual rebels against Rome had reached him. "But our war," declared Octavius, "must be against Cleopatra. Antony is not worthy of being named as an opponent." Then he added with contempt, "He is no more than a slave, the Queen of Egypt's slave."

Antony and Cleopatra now moved with their assembled legions to Actium where their joint fleets were based. This was a port in Greece which looked across the Ionian Sea toward Italy.

The two great armies were gathered, one from the East and one from the West, on opposite shores. Octavius had 100,000 men, and Antony and Cleopatra about the same. Each had a fleet of over 400 ships. In numbers they appeared evenly matched. Octavius' legions were well prepared. His officers and men reflected discipline and training. The same could not be said of Antony's troops. Their commander had been too much occupied with Cleopatra. But his spirits were high and he was sure of victory. The whole world now waited for the outcome of what lay ahead. He would not disappoint them. His faith in his capacity as a commander was absolute.

The night before the first battle, Cleopatra stood in the doorway of Antony's tent. She had consulted her Egyptian fortunetellers. They assured her all the omens were favorable.

But as she looked up at the clear night sky, she suddenly saw a sight that seemed to turn her heart to stone. A single bright star streaked through the sky. Down, down it plunged—a dancing, whirling flame that crashed into the horizon and disappeared.

CHAPTER XXIII

The Battle at Sea

Octavius had begun to move his troops across the sea to the Grecian coast north of Antioch. There in a mighty land battle, the issue between the two rivals could be decided. But when Antony and his generals prepared to get ready for this, Cleopatra raised strong objections. She would not, she said, let her troops or her ships move farther north. Defeat for their side would isolate her dangerously. She was already very far from Egypt. As an ally who was contributing sixty ships and many men to the venture she was entitled to a voice in the decision.

What she perhaps did not express but must have felt was her anxiety about what lay ahead. Antony's army was large but not well organized. Food supplies were low. The leaders and commanders under Antony belonged to a dozen races and nations. Quarrels between them were frequent. Antony's grip on the situation had not reflected the strength he once had.

To the dismay of his generals, who were men accustomed to fighting on land, Antony agreed with Cleopatra. He decided to engage the enemy at sea. They would attack Octavius' fleet near the Grecian coastline and there destroy it.

From the standpoint of numbers, this did not seem to be such a bad idea. Octavius had about four hundred vessels. The combined fleet of Antony included over five hundred ships, some of them tremendous. Unfortunately they proved to be clumsy and hard to maneuver. The ships of Octavius were small but fast.

To make things worse for Antony and Cleopatra, many of their crews had been depleted by illness. The replacements were mostly soldiers and landsmen, unaccustomed to the sea. Men who had never before handled an oar were put to row in the war galleys.

In disagreement with Antony's strategy, some of his generals went over to the other side before the great encounter took place. But this did not turn Antony from his determination to settle the contest at sea. He ordered every ship to take as many troops as could be carried. Then when the enemy craft were rammed and boarded, they could be all the more quickly overwhelmed.

Perhaps no critical battle was ever undertaken so rashly. Antony was a soldier of the land, not of the sea. Ten thousand infantry and twelve thousand horsemen waited his command on shore. But they were left to wait, while he undertook this mad adventure. His confidence in himself and his contempt for the still young Octavius blinded him to reality. More than anything, the word and will of the Queen of Egypt governed him.

On a stormy sea and in the misty dawn of September 2, 31 B.C. the two armadas met near what is now the island of Corfu. Octavius' fast and well-handled ships began to ram the clumsy ships of the enemy al-

most at will. Then with flaming pitch they set fire to
them before Octavius' fighting men could come along-
side for boarding. It was like a cavalry charge against
infantry. Nor was there any naval genius or brilliant
leader aboard to save the day.

Cleopatra, watching with terror from her flagship,
suddenly signaled her own ships to withdraw while
there was still time. They were in the rear of the battle and could successfully disengage. In the high wind
that was blowing, they turned to follow her as she instructed her captain to head home for Egypt.

She also signaled to Antony that she was going.
When he saw this, to the amazement of his own

officers, he abandoned his own ship and followed her in a fast little sailing craft which quickly overtook the Queen's vessel. Once on board Cleopatra's flagship, he made no effort to change its course. Instead, he went forward to the prow and sat there with head bowed as the ship plunged through rough seas on its way to Alexandria. Behind him he left the echoes and horrors of one of the worst major defeats in recorded history, still known as the Battle of Actium.

But Cleopatra wasted no time in regret. She tried to think of what was best to do now. She knew that she must make the decisions. Antony was no longer capable. Shattered by his dreadful defeat, he stayed in the open prow of Cleopatra's ship day and night through the long voyage to Egypt. He spoke to no one, including the Queen.

It was three weeks before they reached port. Since news traveled slowly in those days, no tidings of Actium had reached Alexandria. Antony and Cleopatra were welcomed as conquerers. The luxury and safety of the palace lifted their spirits. Antony slowly revived his hopes and plans. The Queen immediately went to work on hers. She knew it was a mere question of time before fate caught up with them. How soon it would come, she could not guess. But she had to prepare to protect her son and herself and, if possible, her country.

First, she had several small ships moved by land across the Isthmus of Suez to the Red Sea. They were to wait there for her in case there was need for quick escape. The day would come when Octavius would land in Egypt. She must be ready to deal with that emergency.

When these ships were once anchored in the Red Sea, Caesarion would board one of them. It was the plan that he would proceed at once to the Far East, to India. There he was to make alliances in his mother's behalf. He was now sixteen years old, a clever and charming young man. His mother trusted him completely.

Meanwhile Antony sent to Greece Roman officers who were stationed in Egypt and loyal to him. They were to carry his orders to the army in Greece to cross Macedonia and join Antony somewhere in Asia Minor. But this proved to be a fruitless mission. The great army had broken up. Its commanders were dis-

gusted by what they regarded as Antony's desertion
on the field of battle. More than that, they all now
saw Octavius as too great a threat. The news of Actium had slowly but finally reached all areas of the
Mediterranean. In the eyes of everyone, the sun of
Antony had set.

In fact it was fully expected that Octavius would
move on at once. But he appeared to be in no hurry.
Instead, he went back to Rome to enjoy the celebration of his victory. Then he took steps to tighten
Rome's control of Gaul and Spain. This was forever
troublesome territory.

To Antony every day brought news of former allies
who no longer would promise support. There remained
only one on whom he thought he could count. This
was Herod, King of Judea, a powerful monarch who
was hostile to Octavius. But Herod placed an unexpected price on his aid. He told Antony to kill Cleopatra! His purpose was a double one. Herod and
Cleopatra had long feuded. He assured Antony that
the people of Rome would be delighted to hear of the
death of the woman they hated. They would return to
the support of the man who had killed her—especially
if he delivered Egypt as a gift to Rome.

Herod added that he would then back Antony in all
his dealings with Octavius. To this Antony replied
with the only answer the suggestion deserved—contempt and silence.

Antony's love for Cleopatra and his anxiety about
her now dictated his next action. He sent a message
to Octavius in Rome. In it he offered to leave the
political scene entirely and settle down as a private
citizen in Athens. He would accept total and final de-

feat from his enemy. But he put a price on this humbling of his pride and the loss of his personal rights and property as a Roman citizen. It was that Cleopatra and her children should be left alone to live and rule in their land in peace.

To this communication Antony received no answer from Octavius. Weeks went by. The suspense began to mount in the royal palace in Alexandria. When would the attack come and what would happen when it did?

Octavius loomed as the new master of the world. His very silence terrified the lands that had opposed him on Antony's behalf. They sent envoys and rich gifts to Rome to extend friendship. The entire body of Roman soldiers that had formed under Antony in Greece now joined the Octavian legions. Only those Roman officers and men still stationed in Alexandria remained loyal to their old leader.

Never before had such personal triumph been achieved with so little effort. Octavius' position was not just the result of his own ability and effort; it was the effect of the folly and sad fate of his adversary. The time had now come to deal the final blow.

One year after Actium, Octavius, at the head of eighteen legions, moved against Egypt.

CHAPTER XXIV

The Final View

The news that, at last, the forces of destruction were on their way moved Cleopatra to action. When Octavius arrived at the island of Rhodes, from which he would launch his first assault, he found a message from her awaiting him. She offered to surrender her crown if Caesarion and her other children were allowed to keep theirs.

Octavius replied, agreeing to this with one added provision. He wanted her to have Antony killed and his body delivered to him at once. To this she gave the same answer that Antony had given to Herod— silence and contempt.

From Antony went another message to Octavius. He pointed out that Romans still loyal to him would be fighting Romans under Octavius. To avoid this civil war, Antony proposed that Octavius meet him in a personal duel to the death. The answer quickly came that Octavius had better plans for the death of Antony.

From the shores of the Red Sea at the Isthmus of Suez came more bad news. The ships of Cleopatra which were waiting there to take her to India in case of need were burned to the water line by Arabs. But she was reassured by the tidings that Caesarion had safely reached Ethiopia, far from Roman influence.

The legions of Octavius began landing at Pelusium on the Egyptian coast. This was where Pompey had been murdered by Ptolemy's men years before. And there too had landed the Roman reserves that gave Caesar victory in the Alexandrian war. From Pelusium it was not many miles across the Nile delta to Alexandria. Again Roman history was to be written on this flat, sun-baked land.

Antony, stirred from despair into activity, organized his defense. Some Roman infantry and cavalry, as well as Egyptian forces, still remained to him. A first brush with Octavian cavalry gave him success and heightened morale. But the Roman landings at Pelusium continued.

Now for the first time the people of Alexandria saw that a curious addition was being made to the Temple of Aphrodite near the harbor. Workmen were erecting a large domelike building with no windows and no doors. When it was completed, there was an opening on top which gave entrance. Cleopatra was building a tomb for herself! Like the early kings who built pyramids to be buried in, Cleopatra erected for herself this strange mausoleum. But she would not wait to die before being buried in it. She would enter it as soon as it was ready.

Night and day the workmen slaved to complete their task. Meanwhile the fighting on the delta continued. With far fewer troops, Antony was still showing his military talent. Octavius' general, Agrippa, who led the Roman forces, found more spirit in the opposition than he had expected. But every day brought him a bit closer to the walls of Alexandria.

The Queen was now ready to enter her remarkable new home. But before doing so she ordered that all the royal treasure of Egypt be placed in it. Priceless mounds of gold and precious stones, ivory and art objects were lowered through the single opening in the high domed roof. For three days and nights the unloading and storing of all the wealth of Egypt went on.

When that was completed, workmen were lowered by ropes into the building, where they placed a mass of inflammable material. A tinder spark could now instantly ignite a frightful fire. In that fire all the treasure would be totally destroyed.

When these preparations were completed Cleopatra, attended by Charmian and Iras, entered a special apartment that had been prepared for her. All that she possessed in the world was in this tomb with her. She knew well that Octavius longed to put his hands on this vast hoard. She planned to destroy it along with herself unless she could come to terms with him.

The Queen's pressing desire was to save her kingdom for her children and to keep herself from being sent a prisoner to Rome. Her memory of the sight of her sister Arsinoë in chains and rage during Caesar's triumph was engraved on her mind. She had no intention of being dragged after the chariot of Octavius in the same way. She now sent a message to Octavius that might lead to a truce between them before all was lost.

Cleopatra's instincts were correct. In addition to the final defeat and death of Antony, Octavius wanted two things above all. He wanted the living body of Cleopatra to take back to Rome as a prize to be torn apart by the Roman mobs. He also wanted to get his hands on the fabulous fortune that Cleopatra had carried with her into her mausoleum.

The final fight between the forces of Antony and those of Octavius was scarcely a fight. Antony's Roman troops heard that the Egyptians had stopped fighting as soon as they learned of Cleopatra's retirement into her house of death. They realized that further warfare would accomplish nothing. In the open fields outside Alexandria, they went over to the other side. Octavius entered the city without the loss of a man.

The rumor that the Queen was dead came to Antony as Roman forces were surging into the city. His grief at this news overwhelmed him. He begged an aide to run a sword through him. When that was refused, he attempted to put a sword into himself. His wound was mortal but for a time he continued to live.

Then a message came from Cleopatra telling him that she was still alive. He begged Apollodorus to take him to her that he might die by her side. With great difficulty this was done. By ropes he was lowered painfully through the narrow doorway in the dome and carried from there to the Queen's small apartment.

Cleopatra knelt beside him. She held his hand and spoke to him softly. Antony listened to the voice that had so bewitched him, begging him to live, telling him of her love. He opened his eyes. He saw her face as she bent over him. She seemed more beautiful than he had ever seen her.

He knew the end was near. He made a vast effort. He spoke softly to her with his last breath. "I am dying, Egypt," he said.

Cleopatra stayed beside him weeping until Apollodorus covered Antony's body with his cloak. Iras and Charmian took the Queen into another room.

Octavius himself reached the Temple of Aphrodite the following day. He pretended that, with Antony dead, he would now negotiate with Cleopatra as she wished. He pledged his honor as a Roman that no harm would befall her or her children. He said that Egypt would retain its independence and that only the lands that Antony had given her would be taken back by Rome.

To Cleopatra the honor of a Roman was a pledge she had to trust. There was nothing else upon which she could rely to make her world safe for Caesarion. With some reluctance she left her tomb and went back to her quarters in the palace. Octavius told her she would be accorded full royal honors by his troops, and so she was—even to the extent of having guards around her apartment. The guards, he said, were there to protect her. But almost immediately she knew she was a prisoner. No one could enter except her servants and food bearers.

From her window over the harbor, she could see a fast sailing vessel moored. There was great activity aboard, and the Queen asked her young guard officer about it. Perhaps without thinking, perhaps because like other Romans before him he had fallen in love with this lovely woman, he said gently, "It is the ship that will carry you back to Rome."

Now she knew the truth. She knew she had been betrayed.

"When is it due to sail?" she asked.

"Tomorrow, my lady," he answered.

The time had come to act. She knew exactly what

to do. She summoned her Sicilian slave. "I should like some fresh figs, Apollodorus," she said.

He nodded silently and went. He was too sad to speak. For several weeks at the Queen's command he had been testing a variety of poisons. He had learned that the bite of an asp caused the quickest and most painless death. The order that Cleopatra had given him was to fetch for her, concealed from the guards, the serpent he had been keeping for such a moment.

Cleopatra went to the window and looked out for the last time at the harbor and the sea over which she had sailed. She thought of herself as a child sitting on the ledge of a palace window looking at this very scene. She saw again the purple sails billowing in the wind that had carried her to Caesar and again to Antony. She saw Caesarion, a baby in her arms. She remembered the purple tent from which she had gone with Apollodorus to find Caesar. That was the beginning of it all. This was the end.

Apollodorus came back into the room. He had easily passed the guards bearing for the Queen a small basket of fresh figs. He handed it to her. Behind him stood Charmian and Iras. She looked at the three of them. They had shared so much with her, the triumphs and defeats, the sorrow and the happiness.

They returned her look with sad and terrified eyes. She rested for a moment on a couch, then she reached for the basket. Her expression was soft and relaxed for the first time in many weeks.

"Good-by, dear and faithful friends," she said. Then she reached under the figs as eagerly as she had once reached for the world. When she withdrew her hand there was in it a small and shining snake. She

held it close to her body and instantly the vicious creature bit her twice.

There was a wait as the very daylight seemed to leave the room.

"I wish to be buried with Mark Antony," she said.

Then she died. The day was the thirty-first of August in the year 30 B.C. Cleopatra was thirty-nine years old. Her death was a double victory. She would never walk in chains behind a Roman chariot. She would never learn that Caesarion died, strangled on orders from Octavius. There was, he said, no room on earth for two Caesars.

She would never know that her beloved land was made into a Roman province, which it remained for centuries. She would never know that Octavius would soon become the first Emperor of the Roman Empire under the name of Augustus Caesar.

The world has changed in the long and many years since Cleopatra ruled Egypt. But the ancient land is still there. In the desert the pyramids amaze people today as they did Caesar and Cleopatra. There is still a city called Alexandria although the white marble of Cleopatra's city has long crumbled into dust. The Mediterranean Sea is still blue, and the Nile flows on. In the desert the sands which were battlefields are blowing in the hot, dry wind.

The secret source of the Nile was discovered at last about a century ago. No one has yet solved the riddle of the Sphinx. Nor has there ever been another—in all the world—like the extraordinary and beautiful girl who became Cleopatra of Egypt.

Bibliography

The following sources have been consulted profitably and enjoyably by me during the writing of this book:

PLUTARCH'S LIVES (*Modern Library edition*)
CLEOPATRA, *Story of a Queen, by Emil Ludwig*
LIFE OF CLEOPATRA, *by Arthur Weigall*
CLEOPATRA, *Her Life & Reign, by Desire de Bernath*
CLEOPATRA, *A Royal Voluptuary, by Oskar Von Wertheimer*
CLEOPATRA, *by Claude Ferval*
THE IDES OF MARCH, *by Thornton Wilder*
JULIUS CAESAR, *A Landmark Book by John Gunther*
JULIUS CAESAR, *A play by William Shakespeare*
ANTONY AND CLEOPATRA, *A play by William Shakespeare*
CAESAR AND CLEOPATRA, *A play by Bernard Shaw*
ATLAS OF WORLD HISTORY, *Rand-McNally*
THE ENCYCLOPAEDIA BRITANNICA

Index

Index